STANDING BETWEEN YOUR AMEN & HALLELUJAH

31 DAYS OF PERSEVERING IN FAITH AND OVERCOMING THE STORMS OF LIFE

MICHAEL VIDAURRI, D. MIN.

Betty Jo,
We aren't those who draw
back & quit / give up (Heb. 10:39)
We are faith people / covenant
people who press on until we
have recieved the promise
blessings.
Mike Vidaurri

AUTHOR'S NOTE: Some names of persons mentioned in this book have been changed to protect privacy; any similarity between individuals described in this book to individuals known to readers is purely coincidental.

Foreword

In this life of faith we all encounter life-changing, character building, faith stretching experiences. At some point, we come face-to-face with a Judas or a Peter, an Elijah, or an Abraham, a wilderness or a Red Sea experience.

Each of these people experienced times when their faith was challenged and hope was lost. They faced the same challenges you and I face: hardships, disappointments, betrayals, fears, doubts, lack, and loss, yet everyone other than Judas, never took his eyes off of God or His promises.

When I thought about this book and the central theme woven through its pages—the unwavering determination and faith to fight the "Good Fight of Faith" and to trust God no matter what we are facing, it reminded me of the spiritual law of "sowing and reaping."

When we sow a seed, we don't see what's taking place underground—deep within the soil. Before we ever see any signs of life, before we ever get to enjoy the fruit or the byproduct of what's inside of that seed—the seed goes through a process that is unseen by our natural eyes. In fact, that growth takes place hidden beneath the deep, dark, fertile soil.

The law of faith is similar to the process of seed sown beneath the fertile soil, in that we must believe God even when we don't see anything happening in the natural. We must continue to believe that God is bringing about our victory and our breakthrough in spite of the things we see and feel with our five physical senses. After all, each of us is a seed planted in God's garden (His Kingdom). And He has planted us in the earth to produce fruit—but there is a germination process that takes place with every seed that is planted whether natural or spiritual. This process is a type of dying or a stretching of our faith, patience, and our determination to walk in love—even when we don't want to.

Life is riddled with opportunities to give up and allow fear to rob us of our faith. It's during these times that the real fight of faith takes place. It oftentimes seems as if God isolates us before He elevates us. Yet, in the heat of the battle, we must learn to stand like David, and boldly declare, "Today the LORD will help me defeat you." (1 Samuel 17:46, CEV).

When you don't have the means to pay your rent and the threat of eviction is looming over you, fear will try to weasel its way in and become your constant companion. But you must understand that fear is a toxic disease, seeking only to steal, kill, and to destroy you. Fears main goal is to convince us to doubt God's character and to try to convince us to second guess the promises of God by asking us the question, *"Did God really say…?"* (See Genesis 3:1).

It's during these times that our faith in the incorruptible Word of God must rise up out of our spirit and out of our mouths! But in order for God's covenant promises to come out—they must already be planted on the inside of our heart. That's why daily study of the Bible and a habit of meditating on God's promises is so vital. The Bible says that faith comes by hearing and hearing by the Word of God (See Romans 10:17).

I have made it a habit to write down Bible promises and to speak them over myself, my family, and my circumstances repeatedly. I've even spoken God's covenant promises into a tape recorder so that I can have them playing in my ear while I am working on other things throughout the day. The Bible promises us God's Word won't return void. When there is a constant flow of the Word coming into our spirit man—it causes a transformation to take place in the spiritual and physical atmospheres of our lives.

Though I recommend that you put these things to practice in your own life, I am the first to admit that there is a price that comes with living a life of bold faith. That price sometimes includes looking like a fool to those around you.

People who don't have a clear understanding of what faith is, will oftentimes watch you, mock you, and gossip about you. But regardless, STAND strong in the LORD and in the power of His might! (See Ephesians 6:10). Forget about your reputation because it's meaningless.

The Bible says, "But the natural man does not receive the things of the Spirit of God, for they are foolishness to him; nor can he know them, because they are spiritually discerned." (1 Corinthians 2:14, NKJV).

No matter how much turbulence you're facing right now, GOD is with you and He will NEVER leave you or forsake you! God hasn't forgotten you nor has He changed His mind about YOU. You are His blood-bought, covenant child, and He is madly in love with YOU! "He who is the glory of Israel does not lie or change his mind; for he is not a human being, that she should change his mind (1 Samuel 15:29, NIV).

When life is at its worst that's when you need to intensify your praying, continue in your praising; and refuse to relent in your worship of God. Keep on declaring and decreeing God's Word out loud over your life, family, finances, health, and every seemingly negative and destructive thing that is coming your way. And above all, do whatever He tells you to do! Never let people or the enemy rob you of your amen or your hallelujah!

Even though your present situation may look bleak at the moment, God has promised, "Weeping may endure for a night, but joy comes in the morning." (Psalm 30:5).

Moreover, 2 Corinthians 4:17-18 (NLT) says, "[17] For our present troubles are small and won't last very long. Yet they produce for us a glory that vastly outweighs them and will last forever! [18] So we don't look at the troubles we can see now; rather, we fix our gaze on things that cannot be seen. For the things we see now will soon be gone, but the things we cannot see will last forever."

God's promises will never fail. His Word won't return void in your life. Determine to be one of those who will confidently declare, "Even though I walk through the darkest valley, I will fear no evil, for you are with me; your rod and staff, they comfort me" (See Psalm 23:4, NIV).

Stand with God! Trust Him for your deliverance, your peace, your wholeness, and your breakthrough! God is faithful and He will bring you through into victory. Praise your way through the storms of life and never give up while you are *Standing Between Your Amen and Hallelujah!*

Yvonne Carson, M. Div.
Author of: *How to Discover Your Life Purpose and Stop Just Existing ~ A Christian Woman's Guide to Living Life With Purpose, Passion, and Fulfillment*
www.yvonnecarson.com

Introduction

The Apostle Paul instructs believers in Ephesians 6:10-18 (ERV) to, "[10] …Be strong in the Lord and in his great power. [11] Wear the full armor of God. Wear God's armor so that you can fight against the devil's clever tricks. [12] Our fight is not against people on earth. We are fighting against the rulers and authorities and the powers of this world's darkness. We are fighting against the spiritual powers of evil in the heavenly places. [13] That is why you need to get God's full armor. Then on the day of evil, you will be able to stand strong. And when you have finished the whole fight, you will still be standing. [14] So stand strong with the belt of truth tied around your waist, and on your chest wear the protection of right living. [15] On your feet wear the Good News of peace to help you stand strong. [16] And also use the shield of faith with which you can stop all the burning arrows that come from the Evil One. [17] Accept God's salvation as your helmet. And take the sword of the Spirit—that sword is the teaching of God. [18] Pray in the Spirit at all times. Pray with all kinds of prayers, and ask for everything you need. To do this you must always be ready. Never give up. Always pray for all of God's people."

This life we are living in the earth is a fight of faith. In fact, Paul calls it the "Good Fight of Faith." A "Good Fight," is one that WE WIN! And in Jesus we have the promise of VICTORY over the Curse, over sickness and disease, and ultimately over death—HALLELUJAH!

But if we are going to be victorious in life, we must first receive Jesus as our personal Lord and Savior, dare to believe His Word, and STAND on His promises. Quitting is not an option no matter how difficult the battle may be.

When YOU are standing between the AMEN of your prayer and Your HALLELUJAH or the MANIFESTATION of your VICTORY—YOUR **ONLY** responsibilities are to trust God, speak the Word, remain in an attitude of faith and thanksgiving, and to STAND until you WIN!

Table of Contents

Day 1
Standing Between Your AMEN & HALLELUJAH

"¹³ Therefore take up the whole armor of God, that you may be able to withstand in the evil day, *and having done all, to stand.*¹⁴ *Stand therefore,* having girded your waist with truth, having put on the breastplate of righteousness, ¹⁵ and having shod your feet with the preparation of the gospel of peace; ¹⁶ above all, taking the shield of faith with which you will be able to quench all the fiery darts of the wicked one. ¹⁷ And take the helmet of salvation, and the sword of the Spirit, which is the word of God; ¹⁸ praying always with all prayer and supplication in the Spirit, being watchful to this end with all perseverance and supplication for all the saints."

Ephesians 6:13-18 (Emphasis Added)

How do you react when the battle is raging and the enemy is waging his fiercest attack against you, your loved ones, your finances, or your health? What do you do when all hell has broken loose and all of the signs point to your defeat, ruin, or even death? Your unrelenting determination to remain standing under the pressures you're facing will determine whether or not you survive the storm that is raging around you.

It is our responsibility and right as Kingdom citizens to stand and receive our victory in EVERY battle we encounter. But victory doesn't always come immediately—it sometimes comes after we "feel" like we've been battered, bruised, and abused by the enemy. The Good News however, is that if we refuse to give-up and quit—we are promised the victory.

2 Corinthians 2:14 (ERV) says, "But we thank God who gives us the victory through our Lord Jesus Christ!" I don't care how difficult the battle we're facing "feels," we have a promise from Almighty God that He will bring us through every storm–Triumphant!

We have been called to **STAND!** Standing is the unwavering confidence and determination to keep fighting the *"Good Fight Of Faith,"* knowing that God is <u>**ALWAYS**</u> faithful to His covenant promises.

James 1:2-8 says, "²My brethren, count it all joy when you fall into various trials, ³ knowing that the testing of your faith produces patience. ⁴ But let patience have its perfect work, that you may be perfect and complete, lacking nothing. ⁵ If any of you lacks wisdom, let him ask of God, who gives to all liberally and without reproach, and it will be given to him. ⁶ But let him ask in faith, with no doubting, for he who doubts is like a wave of the sea driven and tossed by the wind. ⁷ For let not that man suppose that he will receive anything from the Lord; ⁸ he is a double-minded man, unstable in all his ways."

In 1 Thessalonians 5:24 (AMP) we are told, "Faithful is He Who is calling you [to Himself] and utterly trustworthy, and He will also do it [fulfill His call by hallowing and keeping you]."

The Message Bible says it this way, "The One who called you is completely dependable. If he said it, he'll do it!"

We've got to come to the realization that God is for us, He loves us, and He will never leave us or forsake us. One of my favorite Scriptures is Hebrews 13:5-6 (AMP) which tells us, "⁵…for He [God] Himself has said, I will not in any way fail you nor give you up nor leave you without support. [I will] not, [I will] not, [I will] not in any degree leave you helpless nor forsake nor let [you] down (relax My hold on you)! [Assuredly not!] ⁶ So we take comfort and are encouraged and confidently and boldly say, The Lord is my Helper; I will not be seized with alarm [I will not fear or dread or be terrified]. What can man do to me?"

When we are in the heat of battle, we don't ignore or pretend that everything is fine, but we persevere in faith knowing that God is right beside us every step of the way. We keep marching like good soldiers with the understanding that war is never pleasant, but victory is ALWAYS sweet. We continue believing and speaking God's Word over ourselves, renewing our mind to His will, recognizing that His Word won't return void in our lives, but will produce exactly what He has promised to us.

Sure, there will be times when our flesh will want to throw in the towel and give-up. That's because pressure is painful and our flesh likes to be comforted not stretched or exercised. But we need to understand that when the pressure that's mounted against us is at its highest intensity — that's when we need to stop and recognize that we are seconds away from our breakthrough.

That's when we need to turn our attention away from how uncomfortable and battle-weary we are, and start focusing our attention on praising God even more boldly! That's when we need to start jumping for joy knowing that Satan is giving his last ditch effort to convince us to accept our defeat — BUT DON'T ACCEPT WHAT DOESN'T BELONG TO YOU — YOU'VE BEEN REDEEMED FROM THE CURSE! (See Galatians 3:13-14).

Even though we may be waiting for our manifestation and though we may not have any earthly evidence that any change has taken place in the natural, we need to keep on praising God anyway, knowing that He will honor His covenant Word.

Numbers 23:19 (GWT) tells us, "God is not like people. He tells no lies. He is not like humans. He doesn't change his mind. When he says something, he does it. When he makes a promise, he keeps it."

When we stand on God's Word instead of accepting the circumstances we're facing as the final verdict for our lives; that tells God that we have put our confidence in Him and not in what we are experiencing in the natural. And when He sees that our faith is in Him, He goes to work making good on what He has promised.

Years ago Jerry Savelle, one of my greatest faith heroes, preached a message titled *What To Do From Amen, To There It Is*. This devotional is meant to be a reminder to us all that we have a responsibility to stand in faith while we are waiting for our answers to prayer. Faith isn't comprised exclusively of asking God to intervene, faith is also doing what He commanded us to do until the promise manifests in this earthly realm.

In his message concerning *How To Get From Amen, to There It Is,* brother Savelle said that there is a cycle that every believer must go through in order to receive their breakthrough. He explained that every spiritual battle begins with a **_PROBLEM_**. That Problem then leads us to **_PRAYER_** founded on the promises of God's Word. When we have prayed and asked God to intervene on our behalf, the proper response to our faith in what we have requested of God leads us to **_PRAISE_** for our answer, even before we have any earthly evidence suggesting that we have received what we have believed and requested of Him. And finally, our Praise leads us to our **_PROVISION_**.

Dr. Savelle says, "Praise before the manifestation is just as important as wood is to fire. You don't say give me some heat and then I'll put in some wood — No, the wood comes first! In the same way, we don't say God, give me a manifestation and then I'll praise You — that's backwards!"

Another hero of mine is Pastor Jentezen Franklin. His book, *The Spirit Of Python*, was a vital instrument that God used to help me out of one of my darkest periods and one of the most fierce spiritual battles I have ever experienced.

Franklin writes,

The devil knows the power of atmosphere. That's why most people are enticed into the wrong atmosphere first before they are ever tempted to sin…You can grow bananas in Jamaica, but not in Alaska. Why? The atmosphere is right for banana growing in Jamaica, but it's not right in Alaska. There's something about the atmosphere of a club — the lights, the music, the dancing — it creates an environment that is right for sin. The atmosphere creates a climate and the climate creates a culture. If the enemy can get you in his culture, he knows he can get you to sin. The same is true with the Holy Spirit: atmosphere is everything. The atmosphere of holiness, purity, praise, worship, prayer, love, and unity attract the Holy Spirit — just as an atmosphere of lust, drunkenness, anger, and hatred attracts demonic spirits. God responds to atmosphere as well. He is everywhere — but He does not manifest His presence equally everywhere. God manifests His presence when the atmosphere is right. He loves the atmosphere of praise and of true worship from His people. The Bible says that God inhabits the praises of His people (See Psalm 22:3). The word *inhabits* means He is enthroned or feels comfortable enough to sit down in the place where the atmosphere is filled with celebration, praise, and worship. When you fill the atmosphere with complaining, fault-finding, and murmuring, it's not inviting to the presence of God. It has quite the opposite effect…Miracles happen when the atmosphere is right. When people begin to respond to the presence of God, He responds to people in greater measure." (See *The Spirit Of Python*, pages 26-28).

When we are going through Hell and in the heat of battle, the last thing our flesh wants to do is to begin praising God! No! Our flesh wants to have its own pity party. It wants to lie down on the ground kicking, screaming, and whining like a baby. But I can promise you that won't get you anywhere, but further into despair and farther from the BREAKTHROUGH you desire.

Even though it will take some REAL FAITH to put down your flesh—YOU CAN DO IT! We even have Biblical proof that it is possible. In fact the Apostle Paul writes, "24 You know that in a race all the runners run, but only one runner gets the prize. So run like that. Run to win! 25 All who compete in the games use strict training. They do this so that they can win a prize—one that doesn't last. But our prize is one that will last forever. 26 So I run like someone who has a goal. I fight like a boxer who is hitting something, not just the air. 27 It is my own body I fight to make it do what I want. I do this so that I won't miss getting the prize myself after telling others about it." (1 Corinthians 9:24-27, ERV).

Faith wages war against the ways of the World and the evil desires of the flesh. Faith is always led by the spirit and not controlled by the corruption of sin. Faith praises God during the good times and also in the storms of life.

Look with me at a few example we have from Scripture regarding those who had the faith to praise God all the way through their storm and into their VICTORY.

In Acts 16:16-34 we read, "16 Now it happened, as we went to prayer, that a certain slave girl possessed with a spirit of divination met us, who brought her masters much profit by fortune-telling. 17 This girl followed Paul and us, and cried out, saying, "These men are the servants of the Most High God, who proclaim to us the way of salvation." 18 And this she did for many days. But Paul, greatly annoyed, turned and said to the spirit, "I command you in the name of Jesus Christ to come out of her." And he came out that very hour. 19 But when her masters saw that their hope of profit was gone, they seized

Paul and Silas and dragged them into the marketplace to the authorities. [20] And they brought them to the magistrates, and said, "These men, being Jews, exceedingly trouble our city; [21] and they teach customs which are not lawful for us, being Romans, to receive or observe." [22] Then the multitude rose up together against them; and the magistrates tore off their clothes and commanded them to be beaten with rods. [23] And when they had laid many stripes on them, they threw them into prison, commanding the jailer to keep them securely. [24] Having received such a charge, he put them into the inner prison and fastened their feet in the stocks. [25] *But at midnight Paul and Silas were PRAYING and SINGING HYMNS TO GOD, and the prisoners were listening to them. [26] Suddenly there was a great earthquake, so that the foundations of the prison were shaken; and immediately all the doors were opened and everyone's chains were loosed.* [27] And the keeper of the prison, awaking from sleep and seeing the prison doors open, supposing the prisoners had fled, drew his sword and was about to kill himself. [28] But Paul called with a loud voice, saying, "Do yourself no harm, for we are all here." [29] Then he called for a light, ran in, and fell down trembling before Paul and Silas. [30] And he brought them out and said, "Sirs, what must I do to be saved?" [31] So they said, "Believe on the Lord Jesus Christ, and you will be saved, you and your household." [32] Then they spoke the word of the Lord to him and to all who were in his house. [33] And he took them the same hour of the night and washed their stripes. And immediately he and all his family were baptized. [34] Now when he had brought them into his house, he set food before them; and he rejoiced, having believed in God with all his household." (Emphasis Added).

Do you see that? The earth shook, the foundations rocked, and the bonds that were restricting Paul and Silas were loosed when they first prayed and then praised God in the midst of their troubles. I cannot guarantee how quickly it will be for you, but I can guarantee that it will happen if you will stir yourself up to pray and praise God in the midst of your storm. Breakthrough will come to you when you are willing to honor God and focus on His goodness and faithfulness in spite of the trials you are facing. Our God is a faith God—He always honors faith and confidence in Him and His precious promises.

Now notice what happened in 2 Chronicles 20:1-26 (NLT). "After this, the armies of the Moabites, Ammonites, and some of the Meunites declared war on Jehoshaphat. ²Messengers came and told Jehoshaphat, "A vast army from Edom is marching against you from beyond the Dead Sea. They are already at Hazazon-tamar." (This was another name for En-gedi.) ³Jehoshaphat was terrified by this news and begged the LORD for guidance. He also ordered everyone in Judah to begin fasting. [**The New King James says,** *"Jehoshaphat feared, and set himself to seek the LORD, and proclaimed a fast throughout all Judah."*] ⁴So people from all the towns of Judah came to Jerusalem to seek the LORD's help. ⁵Jehoshaphat stood before the community of Judah and Jerusalem in front of the new courtyard at the Temple of the LORD. ⁶**He prayed,** "O LORD, God of our ancestors, you alone are the God who is in heaven. You are ruler of all the kingdoms of the earth. You are powerful and mighty; no one can stand against you! ⁷O our God, did you not drive out those who lived in this land when your people Israel arrived? And did you not give this land forever to the descendants of your friend Abraham? ⁸Your people settled here and built this Temple to honor your name. ⁹They said, 'Whenever we are faced with any calamity such as war, plague, or famine, we can come to stand in your presence before this Temple where your name is honored. *We can cry out to you to save us, and you will hear us and rescue us.'* ¹⁰"And now see what the armies of Ammon, Moab, and Mount Seir are doing. You would not let our ancestors invade those nations when Israel left Egypt, so they went around them and did not destroy them. ¹¹Now see how they reward us! For they have come to throw us out of your land, which you gave us as an inheritance. *12 O our God, won't you stop them? We are powerless against this mighty army that is about to attack us. We do not know what to do, but we are looking to you for help."* 13 As all the men of Judah stood before the LORD with their little ones, wives, and children, *14 the Spirit of the LORD came upon one of the men standing there. His name was Jahaziel son of Zechariah, son of Benaiah, son of Jeiel, son of Mattaniah, a Levite who was a descendant of Asaph. 15 He said, "Listen, all you people of Judah and Jerusalem! Listen, King Jehoshaphat! This is what the LORD says: Do not be afraid! Don't be discouraged by this mighty army, for the battle is not yours, but God's.* 16 Tomorrow, march out against them. You will find them coming up through the ascent of Ziz at the end of the valley that opens into the wilderness of Jeruel. *17 But you will not even need to fight. Take your positions; then stand still and watch the LORD's victory. He is with you, O people of Judah and Jerusalem. Do not be afraid or discouraged. Go out against them tomorrow, for the LORD is with you!" 18 Then King Jehoshaphat bowed low with his face to the ground. And all the people of Judah and Jerusalem did the same, worshiping the LORD.* 19 Then the Levites from the clans of Kohath and Korah **stood to praise the LORD**, the God of Israel, with a very loud shout. 20 Early the next morning the army of Judah went out into the wilderness of Tekoa. On the way Jehoshaphat stopped and said, "Listen to me, all you people of Judah and Jerusalem! **Believe in the LORD your God, and you will be able to stand firm. Believe in his prophets, and you will succeed." 21 After consulting the people, the king appointed singers to walk ahead of the army, singing to the LORD and praising him for his holy splendor.** This is what they sang: "Give thanks to the LORD; his faithful love endures forever!" *22 At the very moment they began to sing and give praise, the LORD caused the armies of Ammon, Moab, and Mount Seir to start fighting among themselves.* 23 The armies of Moab and Ammon turned against their allies from Mount Seir and killed every one of them. After they had destroyed the army of Seir, they began attacking each other. [24] So when the army of Judah arrived at the lookout point in the wilderness, all they saw were dead bodies lying on the ground as far as they could see. *Not a single one of the enemy had escaped.* [25] King Jehoshaphat and his men went out to gather the plunder. They found vast amounts of equipment, clothing, and other valuables — more than they could carry. There was so much plunder that it took them three days just to collect it all! [26] *On the fourth day they gathered in the <u>VALLEY OF BLESSING,</u> which got its name that day because the people praised and thanked the LORD there.* It is still called the Valley of Blessing today." (Emphasis Added).

If you want to move from Amen to Hallelujah, if you want to move from the heat of battle to the Valley of Blessing, it is going to depend on what you do when you are plowing your way through the storms of life.

Prayer and Praise built on the promises of the Word will take you where you want to go — as long as you don't give -up! God has promised you the Victory, but whether or not you get there depends on whose report you believe and how hard you're willing to fight the Good Fight of Faith to get what God has promised to you.

The choice is yours — when you are STANDING BETWEEN YOUR AMEN & HALLELUJAH — Praise God and He will lead you into your Victory! He will NEVER leave you or forsake you. He is our faithful God.

Daily Declaration

Heavenly Father, I thank You for going before me, behind me, and for surrounding me with Your FAVOR, as a shield in all I do. (See Psalm 5:12). Your Word promises me that You will never leave me or forsake me (See Hebrews 13:5-6). I know that to be true—You are my faithful God!

Even in the midst of the storms, I can rest assured and cast my cares upon You, because You care for me. Father, my complete faith is in Jesus—Your Son! He is my salvation and You are my refuge and strength.

Like the Psalmist I will praise Your name saying, "[1] God is our refuge and strength, an ever-present help in trouble. [2] Therefore we will not fear, though the earth give way and the mountains fall into the heart of the sea, [3] though its waters roar and foam and the mountains quake with their surging." (Psalm 46:1-3, NIV).

You Lord, have given me salvation through Jesus—and that salvation includes wholeness, safety, protection, prosperity, and every "Good Thing" which You planned for me from the foundation of the earth.

I boldly declare, "[1] The LORD is my light and my salvation—whom shall I fear? The LORD is the stronghold of my life—of whom shall I be afraid? [2] When the wicked advance against me to devour me, it is my enemies and my foes who will stumble and fall. [3] Though an army besiege me, my heart will not fear; though war break out against me, even then I will be confident." (Psalm 27:1-3, NIV). I pray all these things in the mighty name of Jesus, Amen.

Day 2
Fasting Your Way To Breakthrough

"[16] Moreover, when you fast, do not be like the hypocrites, with a sad countenance. For they disfigure their faces that they may appear to men to be fasting. Assuredly, I say to you, they have their reward. [17] But you, when you fast, anoint your head and wash your face, [18] so that you do not appear to men to be fasting, but to your Father who is in the secret place; and your Father who sees in secret will reward you openly."

Matthew 6:16-18

How hungry are you for God's anointing, favor, and Blessing? I want to share something that has absolutely revolutionized my life and become a regular part of my worship over the past few years — FASTING. Now before you get depressed and start complaining about how you have tried to fast in the past and failed, or start whining about how it's impossible for YOU to fast let me share some Bible and personal stories that I hope will encourage you in your endeavors.

We all understand the power of faith, the power of prayer, and many of us are familiar with the power of sowing — or the Blessing that accompanies the lifestyle of being a generous giver. But many Christians have never noticed that Jesus told us to not only pray and give of ourselves and our finances, but He also instructed us to fast.

It is clear from Scripture that Jesus expected us to do all three of those things (pray, give, and fast). Notice what He says in Matthew 6:2-8 and then in Matthew 6:16. In both of these passages Jesus says, "When you give, when you pray, when you fast..."

I think most Christians have overlooked an important part of the life of faith that Jesus has clearly outlined in Scripture, and in doing so, they have lost out on part of the anointing, supernatural favor, and Blessing that is available to them.

In Matthew 6:2-8, 16-18 (NLT) we read, "2 ***When you give*** to someone in need, don't do as the hypocrites do—blowing trumpets in the synagogues and streets to call attention to their acts of charity! I tell you the truth, they have received all the reward they will ever get. 3 But when you give to someone in need, don't let your left hand know what your right hand is doing. 4 Give your gifts in private, and your Father, who sees everything, will reward you. 5 "***When you pray***, don't be like the hypocrites who love to pray publicly on street corners and in the synagogues where everyone can see them. I tell you the truth, that is all the reward they will ever get. 6 But when you pray, go away by yourself, shut the door behind you, and pray to your Father in private. Then your Father, who sees everything, will reward you. 7 "When you pray, don't babble on and on as people of other religions do. They think their prayers are answered merely by repeating their words again and again. 8 Don't be like them, for your Father knows exactly what you need even before you ask him!... 16 "And ***When you fast***, don't make it obvious, as the hypocrites do, for they try to look miserable and disheveled so people will admire them for their fasting. I tell you the truth, that is the only reward they will ever get. [17] But when you fast, comb your hair and wash your face. [18] Then no one will notice that you are fasting, except your Father, who knows what you do in private. And your Father, who sees everything, will reward you."

It is clear from this passage that Jesus expects us to give, He expects us to pray, and we are expected to fast from time to time. With these expectations in mind, I believe that we all need to do some introspection and then honestly determine how well we are following through with His commands.

Don't get me wrong, I don't think we need to become legalistic about our fasting, but if the Lord expects us to fast, then it should definitely be part of our lifestyle of faith.

In Matthew 17:18-21, Jesus illustrates a secret to our Kingdom Authority, "[18] And Jesus rebuked the demon, and it came out of him; and the child was cured from that very hour. [19] Then the disciples came to Jesus privately and said, "Why could we not cast it out?" [20] So Jesus said to them, "Because of your unbelief; for assuredly, I say to you, if you have faith as a mustard seed, you will say to this mountain, 'Move from here to there,' and it will move; and nothing will be impossible for you. [21] *__However, this kind does not go out except by prayer and fasting.__*"

You see there are some demonic obstacles that are trying to hold us back and keep us out of our God-ordained Promised Land. And these spiritual strongholds require a deeper level of power and anointing to break us through and carry us over into the victory side of life.

That is exactly what Jesus said in Matthew 17:21, prayer is powerful and can move mountains when faith is applied to it, but some circumstances we come up against also need the supernatural power that only comes from prayer which is coupled and energized by fasting—giving up the natural for God's supernatural. I have experienced this over and over in my own life.

The first time I fasted purposefully was when I was a student at Oral Robert's University. I was in my early thirties and faced with some very big decisions. There were some circumstances that looked impossible to overcome in the natural realm. I had always heard that fasting makes hearing from God easier and that He pours out His Blessing upon them.

I decided that no matter how difficult, I was going to trust God for my miracle and spend the next few days praying, fasting, and seeking God for my answer.

The first three days were quiet. I prayed and fasted, but never heard God speak a word. However, the strangest thing began to happen. Every morning at 1:19 a.m., I would wake up sensing that I should go down stairs and pray. I would quietly get out of bed so that I didn't wake my wife or children, and then go down stairs to read my Bible and pray in the Spirit. After some time in the Word and praying in the Spirit, I would then begin praying and praising God in English, thanking Him for His provision, His goodness, and His answers to my prayers. When I was finished, I would sit there quietly waiting to hear God speak to me—but nothing.

On the fourth morning I was awoke at 1:19 a.m. and went down stairs and began praying. Immediately a flood of words and sentences began filling my spirit. I grabbed a pen and paper and began writing it all down, not sure what I was writing. When it was all over, in what seemed to me like about five minutes, I had three pages of things God had spoken into my spirit which set the ground work for Patty and me to move back to California to plant our first church.

I had no idea how we were going to afford the move, how we were going to afford to live in the areas of California that I believed God was calling us to—BUT GOD DID.

I was hesitant to say anything to Patty about what I had experienced because I thought; she is going to think I was crazy. After all, I was having second thoughts about what had just occurred and was wondering if I was crazy or if I had just somehow gotten myself so fired up about what others had told me would happen when I fasted that I subconsciously made the thing up in my mind?

But God always confirms His Word to us either through His Word, people, or by revelation knowledge that _ALWAYS_ lines up with Scripture.

A few days after hearing from God, I received a call from a friend I used to work with before moving to Tulsa. He called to ask if I'd consider coming back to the pharmaceutical company I'd left to attend ORU. I politely thanked him, but turned him down, only to be told to hush and to listen to his proposal before making my decision.

Earlier that week, I'd come home and found Patty on the internet looking at homes in San Luis Obispo, California which was one of the two places I believed God was calling us to plant churches.

As my friend made his offer, he agreed to pay for all of our moving expenses back to California, and added, "I have three territories open right now and wanted to see if you'd be willing to come back and take one of them." He followed those words by saying, "I have Fresno, San Luis Obispo, and Monterey available."

On the night that I believed God had spoken to me, He said, "I want you to plant churches in San Luis Obispo and Monterey, California.

My friend also promised a sign on bonus and a larger salary than I had before leaving the company to attend ORU. God had miraculously moved the mountains that stood between me and what I believed He had called me to do. He'd opened doors that were otherwise impossible to open before. I truly believe this all took place because I sensed in my spirit the need to fast, pray, and seek God for an answer to a situation I was facing.

The same thing happened when we moved to Tennessee. We knew that we were supposed to move and plant another church here, but neither of us had a job, we didn't have a place to stay, our finances were very tight, but God said go so we went.

Before I announced to our church that we were leaving California and moving to Tennessee I felt led to embark on a 21 day fast. I wanted to make sure what I was sensing in my spirit was really God.

It was heartbreaking to think about leaving the church we had planted in California. We had put everything we had into planting it — all of our heart, our energy, finances and we loved those people like family. I felt like I would be leaving a part of me behind and like I was betraying those who had put their trust in me — my heart was breaking and I struggled to obey God.

I couldn't understand why He would ask me to leave California and move almost 3000 miles away to start another church, when we hadn't finished what He'd asked us to do here? The only thing I was sure of was that God said go — so we packed up a few things and left, trusting that God would make the way as He'd always done before.

When we arrived in Nashville we stayed with family for a couple of days, but quickly wore out our welcome. A few days later one of Patty's friends, who had just moved to Tennessee from Montana, had graciously invited us to stay with her family. But after a couple of weeks we decided that we needed our own space and decided to move into an Extended Stay type of hotel. It was cramped to say the least, two beds in a studio room, but we had a kitchen to prepare our food.

About three weeks after moving into the hotel, I was offered a job working there as the night-time security guard for four hours each night. The job allowed us to live in the hotel rent free and provided a small check every two weeks. I was grateful to God, but had not earned such a puny income since Junior High. Yet I took the job grateful to God for something to move us forward and continued praying and trusting Him for an even better promotion in the near future.

About three months into the hotel job, I was called by a recruiter and offered the opportunity to interview for a medical/pharmaceutical sales position with a Fortune 20 company.

Prior to the interview, I spent a couple of days praying and seeking God about the job. I wanted His guidance because I hadn't moved to Tennessee to go back into sales, but to plant another church. During that time I was asking God to lead me and to help me make the right decisions. If I was supposed to take the job, I wanted to make a good impression during my interview.

The interview was very comfortable. The hiring manager was very polite and kind and I liked her personality from the beginning. About five minutes into our time she asked me a couple of questions that I answered without really thinking beforehand.

One of the questions was, "Are you currently reading any books?" To which I responded, "Oh yes, I'm an avid reader. I'm currently reading a book Glenn Beck has recommended and another that is ministry related." After hearing what had just come out of my mouth, I pinched myself thinking, *Boy if she is not conservative, you just blew this interview by bringing up Glenn Beck AND Christianity.*

A few minutes later she asked what my key priorities would be if she was to hire me on as the Sales Associate for that territory. Again, speaking without really thinking about what I was saying, I answered, "My priorities have always been the same, God always comes first, my family second, and then work and everything else."

I could have kicked myself! Even though my answer was truthful, I had just informed her that work was nowhere near the top of my priorities. And though anyone with half a brain already knows this—they still don't like to hear it. Her last words to me were, "Well we'll be in touch within the next 6 to 8 weeks if you are chosen to move forward. Thank you for your time."

As I got into my car I began praying again before leaving the parking lot. I thanked God for the opportunity and said, "Lord, I feel like I blew this interview. If I am supposed to have this job, You are going to have to somehow fix any mess I may have created."

Down deep I really wanted and needed this job to take care of my family and get us out of the hotel and into a real home and sense of normalcy. I final words before driving home were, "Lord, please don't allow her to get me out of her thoughts and mind, but to remain there in a positive way, in Jesus name."

Two days later I received a call from that same hiring manager who called to say, "Mike, I have interviewed a number of candidates for the open territory, many of whom are more qualified than you. ***BUT FOR SOME REASON, I CAN'T SEEM TO GET YOU OUT OF MY MIND. THEREFORE, I AM CALLING TO OFFER YOU THE POSITION IF YOU WANT IT?***

Tears rolled down my face as she spoke those words through the phone. God had proved Himself faithful once again! I was overwhelmed with joy and surprise. Not that He had honored His Word, but the way He brought it about—this HAD TO BE GOD! He had supernaturally opened doors for me that no man could shut. It certainly wasn't my wonderful interviewing skills that got me the job—IT WAS HIM! I also believe that my time spent in prayer and fasting played a crucial role as well.

Up to that point I had spent months applying for hundreds of jobs with no luck of even receiving a single call back. I had even applied for this exact position on the company's website months earlier, yet the recruiter who called said he never received my resume. He told me that he found my name and resume on a job board and thought I would be a good match.

In Psalm 42:1-3 David writes, "As the deer pants for the water brooks, so pants my soul for You, O God. [2] My soul thirsts for God, for the living God. When shall I come and appear before God? [3] *My tears have been my food day and night*, while they continually say to me, "Where is your God?" (Emphasis added).

In Matthew 4:4 Jesus declares, "It is written, 'Man shall not live by bread alone, but by every word that proceeds from the mouth of God.'"

In Matthew 5:6 Jesus says, "Blessed are those who hunger and thirst for righteousness, for they shall be filled."

And finally in Job 23:12 we read, "I have not departed from the commandment of His lips; *I have treasured the words of His mouth more than my necessary food.*" (Emphasis Added).

There is something amazing that occurs when we give up food for a set period of time to seek God and hear from Heaven. Some things only happen when both prayer and fasting are working in unison. Obstacles that once blocked the way are miraculously torn down. There is something special and intimate that occurs when you are so determined to seek God's face that you sacrifice fleshly needs and desires in order to receive God's best.

When you honor God by devoting yourself to Him, to the Word, to prayer and fasting—nothing can stand in your way. Those seemingly tough demons that once refused to cease and desist will scamper away in fear. You have all of God's ability and the armies of Heaven backing you up.

Moreover, I have found in my own experiences that you do in fact hear God more clearly. All of the outside noises of life are diminished. I encourage you to begin to incorporate fasting as part of your regular worship and experience for yourself. I promise you won't regret it—it will bring Breakthrough into your life like never before.

Fasting isn't meant to be a method used to "twist God's arm," but it's a time to seek Him more intimately and to "tune in," to His will for our lives. God honors His Word and He honors those who will humble themselves before Him and seek Him as their God, Source, and Savior. Be Blessed in Jesus Name!

Daily Declaration

Father, I take dominion over my flesh and over every demonic tactic that the devil would try to use to limit me and keep me from Your best. I am a child of the Most-High God. No weapon formed against me shall prosper — but instead fall to the ground harmless and ineffective against me in Jesus' name. (See Isaiah 54:17).

Holy Spirit I ask for your divine direction and leading concerning all that You would have me to do. I am a willing vessel devoted to Jesus and the call that God has placed on my life. I surrender my will for Yours Father. Your ways, Your plans, Your best is higher and better than anything I could ever dream-up or imagine, because You are madly in love with me. (See Isaiah 55:8-9 and Ephesians 3:20).

Holy Spirit, guide me into all truth. Show me when You would have me to fast. I know that You are not trying to keep me from anything good, but You are trying to get me to the place of BLESSING and FAVOR. And I am willing to sacrifice food for a period of time in order to hear and obey whatever it is that You would have me to do.

In Job 23:12 we read, "I have not departed from the commandment of His lips; I have treasured the words of His mouth more than my necessary food."

David wrote in the Psalms, "How sweet are Your words to my taste, sweeter than honey to my mouth!" (Psalm 119:103).

The Prophet Jeremiah even declared, "When I discovered your words, I devoured them. They are my joy and my heart's delight for I bear your name." (Jeremiah 15:16,

NLT).

Lord I am so hungry for You! I am hungry to hear You speak to my spirit! For I know when You speak to me that I will quickly obey and receive the fullness of Your promise.

Like the Prophet Isaiah I declare that I will seek You, I will find You, I will Hear You speak, and in return I will reply, "Here am I! Send me." I pray all these things in the mighty name of Jesus, Amen.

Day 3
FAITH — Your Title Deed

"¹NOW FAITH is the assurance (the confirmation, the title deed) of the things [we] hope for, being the proof of things [we] do not see and the conviction of their reality [faith perceiving as real fact what is not revealed to the senses]. ²For by [faith — trust and holy fervor born of faith] the men of old had divine testimony borne to them *and* obtained a good report. ³By faith we understand that the worlds [during the successive ages] were framed (fashioned, put in order, and equipped for their intended purpose) by the word of God, so that what we see was not made out of things which are visible."

Hebrews 1:1-3 (AMP)

Years ago people attacked Brother Hagin for a book that he wrote entitled: *Having Faith In Your Faith.* They got mad at him claiming that he was teaching a false doctrine and encouraging people to have faith in themselves instead of faith in God. That is so ridiculous if you think about it, because our faith comes directly from God. The Bible says that He gave to everyone "The Measure Of Faith" (Romans 12:3, KJV), which came directly from Him. It stands to reason that if we could work our own miracles then we wouldn't need to seek God for His help in the first place.

In his book, Brother Hagin taught about the power of faith. He encouraged people as the Apostle James does, to not be double minded, but to stick with the Word of God as their FINAL AUTHORITY and to plow through opposition until they received the manifestation — the object for which they had believed.

James 1:5-8 says, "⁵ If any of you lacks wisdom, let him ask of God, who gives to all liberally and without reproach, and it will be given to him. ⁶ But let him ask in faith, with no doubting, for he who doubts is like a wave of the sea driven and tossed by the wind. ⁷ For let not that man suppose that he will receive anything from the Lord; ⁸ he is a double-minded man, unstable in all his ways."

News Flash—neither you, nor I, are God. We all need His help, His direction, and His wisdom. And those things will only be found in His Word or received by revelation knowledge we receive through prayer. Moreover, if the answer is from God—it will ***ALWAYS*** line up with the teaching of the Bible. God's Word (the Bible), ***IS*** His will for our lives.

If we lack wisdom, James encourages us to ask God and then God will lead and direct us to the answer if we have the faith to believe and are obedient to act on what He has said.

That's what faith is all about. Faith is seeking God for the wisdom we need to overcome any and every obstacle we face and then remaining confident that He will do what He's promised in His Word. Now tell me, is that placing our faith in our abilities or in His?

Notice again what Hebrews 11:1-3 (AMP) says, "¹NOW FAITH is the assurance (the confirmation, the title deed) of the things [we] hope for, being the proof of things [we] do not see and the conviction of their reality [faith perceiving as real fact what is not revealed to the senses]. ² For by [faith—trust and holy fervor born of faith] the men of old had divine testimony borne to them *and* obtained a good report. ³ By faith we understand that the worlds [during the successive ages] were framed (fashioned, put in order, and equipped for their intended purpose) by the word of God, so that what we see was not made out of things which are visible."

There are three points that I believe God wants us to understand from these Scriptures. First, faith is your title deed; it's your proof, your confirmation. If you go on vacation and are checking into a hotel, what do you give the clerk at the hotel registration counter when you check in…Your confirmation number?

That confirmation number proves that you booked a room for your stay. A title deed is the same thing—It proves that something belongs to you.

In spiritual matters; our FAITH proves to the world, to the devil, and to all the Nay Sayers, that what you've believed God for, belongs to you regardless of what they can perceive with their five physical senses.

More importantly, Faith is your lifeline—it connects you to the One who has granted you the right to have what you've believed Him for—and He is faithful and won't ever let you down.

Philippians 1:6 says, "Being confident of this very thing, that He who has begun a good work in you will complete it until the day of Jesus Christ." God has put that desire in your heart and wants you to receive it.

1 Thessalonians 5:23-24 declares, "²³ Now may the God of peace Himself sanctify you completely; and may your whole spirit, soul, and body be preserved blameless at the coming of our Lord Jesus Christ. ²⁴ He who calls you is faithful, who also will do it." In other words, God **_ALWAYS_** makes good on His promises!

The second point that we learn from Hebrews 11:2 is that all of our spiritual forefathers in the faith had a "GOOD REPORT." They were able to tell all of those who made fun of them, all of those who told them that what they had believing for would never come to pass, that they had received what they had believed of God.

That is vitally important in our faith journey. It is a foundation that we can STAND upon when the enemy comes to us and tries to cause us to doubt and give-up. We can point back to them and rend the devil that God is no respecter of persons — if He did it for them, then He will surely do it for us also! (See Acts 10:34 and Romans 2:11).

Jesus is The Good Shepherd (See John 10:11), His name is on the line. If He has promised something in His Word, you can rest assured that His promises will come to pass — it's a done deal.

Romans 10:11 further states, "For the Scripture says, "Whoever believes on Him will not be put to shame."

The third and final point that I want to make from Hebrews 11:3 is that the Word of God is a Creative Force. The Word can and will create, change, alter, or rearrange any and every negative circumstance we face, if we will believe it and have the courage to speak it continually.

It was God's Word that created this planet and the entire universe. The Bible tells us that we have been created in His likeness and have been given His dominion to rule and reign in this world (Genesis 1:26-28).

Whenever words are spoken, they have the power to create. The Hebrew word translated as "words" is *davar*, which means: matter, things, or words. Words ARE THINGS. They are the invisible spiritual containers which create our reality

Proverbs 18:20-21(MSG) says, "[20] Words satisfy the mind as much as fruit does the stomach; good talk is as gratifying as a good harvest. [21] Words kill, words give life; they're either poison or fruit — you choose."

Job 22:28 states, "You will also declare a thing, and it will be established for you; so light will shine on your ways."

Your words matter — they will either give life or death to your dreams and everything else around you. Your words establish, or lay the foundation for your future. When your words are based on God's Word, you will always be a winner, because His Word always gives life. But negative words have the power to destroy and even cause death.

In conclusion, Mark 11:22-24 sums up what we have been talking about, "²²So Jesus answered and said to them, "Have faith in God. ²³ For assuredly, I say to you, whoever says to this mountain, 'Be removed and be cast into the sea,' and does not doubt in his heart, but believes that those things he says will be done, he will have whatever he says. ²⁴ Therefore I say to you, whatever _**things**_ you ask when you pray, believe that you receive _**them**_, [those things you have said], and you will have _**them**_."

When you put your faith in God and in His Word, When you are confident and immoveable in your faith (sure that He will bring it to pass and give you a good report), and when you understand the importance of your words based on the promises of the Bible — _**THEN**_ you are in the perfect position to move mountains and to shake up this world for the glory of God!

Remember — God has already given you the TITLE DEED, the CONFIRMATION, the PROOF that it belongs to you — In HIS WORD — So HAVE FAITH and EXPERIENCE THE BLESSING OF GOD!

Daily Declaration

I declare that no mountain, no problem, no obstacle can stand in my way — in Jesus' name! I am the redeemed of the Lord, and I have been given dominion (the TITLE DEED) to everything Jesus went to the cross to provide for me.

Jesus' blood not only provided for my eternal salvation and forgiveness from sin, but it also paid the full price for my FREEDOM from the Curse and all that is tied to it: Sickness, Death, Fear, Lack, Shame, Depression, and so much more!

I take hold and receive those things by faith — **_ALL_** that Jesus has intended for me to have! I am a Joint-Heir with Christ and I rightfully take my place seated with Him in Heavenly places as a King and Priest of God. (See Romans 8:16-17, Ephesians 2:4-7, and Revelations 1:6).

I declare that I have mountain moving faith! That I receive whatever I say, and that God's goodness and mercy — His Grace — or unmerited and undeserved FAVOR, follows me wherever I go. (See Psalm 23:6).

I know that positive change is already taking place in my life right now! As I speak, I take hold of the TITLE DEED to EVERYTHING that belongs to me as a member of the family of God. I believe I receive it by faith and I declare that it is mine RIGHT NOW — in the mighty name of Jesus, Amen.

Day 4
Ditch The Baggage

"^{31} What shall we say about such wonderful things as these? If God is for us, who can ever be against us? ^{32} Since He did not spare even His own Son but gave Him up for us all, won't He also give us everything else? ...^{38} And I am convinced that nothing can ever separate us from God's love. Neither death nor life, neither angels nor demons, neither our fears for today nor our worries about tomorrow—not even the powers of hell can separate us from God's love."

Romans 8:31-32, 38 (NLT)

I remember when I first dedicated my life to the Lord, I'm not talking about when I was twelve years old and my uncle Terry and my grandmother led me through the prayer of salvation, but when I finally determined that I was tired of trying to do it on my own. I was tired of waking up feeling like someone had kicked me in the head with steel-toed boots, because I had partied so hard the night before. I was tired of trying to work on a marriage that just wasn't getting any better. And I was tired of feeling like I was living a life void of love, joy, peace, and worth.

Boy was I a mess! As stated above, I had gone through the motions of Christianity and had received Jesus as Lord at the age of twelve, but there hadn't been a real heart change on my part. After the excitement wore off and I realized that I needed to make some serious decisions I decided that it wasn't right for me to live a lie and straddle the fence with one leg in the world and the other in the Church.

I enjoyed the sin I was involved in and I refused to be like many of the "Christians" I had despised before giving my life to the Lord, who were "angels" on Sundays, but demons the rest of the week.

Not wanting to be a hypocrite, I decided to jump into my sin with both feet and hoped that one day—before I died, I'd be able to come back to God when I was ready? I am so Blessed that the devil didn't take me out during those dark years. I gave him plenty of opportunities and it is only by God's amazing grace that I am still alive and that I have fully surrendered my life to Him

It wasn't until my mid-twenties that I finally realized I was killing myself. I had succeeded in making money, succeeded in being popular, but failed miserably at really matters: Life, Love, and making a difference in other's lives. Instead of building people up, I spent most of my early life tearing people down through the drugs that I dealt and hurting those who owed me money.

Guilt and shame had become a prison of sorts because of my past. Sure, I wasn't doing those things anymore, but the memories still haunted my waking hours. And yes, I went to church, but I believed that God could never really use me, because of all of the horrible things I had done.

I was convinced that I was finally going to Heaven, but only by the skin of my teeth and only because of God's unfathomable mercy and unmerited favor. But down deep inside, a voice continued to remind me that I was too bad for God to truly be forgive me of my sins—that I was beyond hope and would never amount to anything but the thug I had been in my past.

How many of you have believed this same lie? Did you know that the devil uses the same tactics with everyone — Guilt, Shame, Accusations, and he'll lie to you and tell you that whatever you've done is so bad that God could never forgive you of those sins?

I would have received that lie and remained trapped if it hadn't been for a minister by the name of Jesse Duplantis who was bold enough to stir me to anger with something he said. This guy was not like any other minister I had ever heard. In fact, at first, I thought he was crazy. But as he described his life before Jesus, I began to cry. It was almost an exact replication of my own. His life had been filled with stories of drug abuse, chasing women, chasing money, and hurting people. I absolutely knew that if God could use Jesse Duplantis, He could certainly use me. It wasn't that I thought I was any better than him, but I definitely hadn't been any worse!

I had also discovered Romans 8:1-11 (NLT) which said, "So now there is no condemnation for those who belong to Christ Jesus. [2] And because you belong to him, the power of the life-giving Spirit has freed you from the power of sin that leads to death. [3] The law of Moses was unable to save us because of the weakness of our sinful nature. So God did what the law could not do. He sent his own Son in a body like the bodies we sinners have. And in that body God declared an end to sin's control over us by giving his Son as a sacrifice for our sins. [4] He did this so that the just requirement of the law would be fully satisfied for us, who no longer follow our sinful nature but instead follow the Spirit. [5] Those who are dominated by the sinful nature think about sinful things, but those who are controlled by the Holy Spirit think about things that please the Spirit. [6] So letting your sinful nature control your mind leads to death. But letting the Spirit control your mind leads to life and peace. [7] For the sinful nature is always hostile to God. It never did obey God's laws, and it never will. [8] That's why those who are still under the control of their sinful nature can never please God. [9] But you are not controlled by your sinful nature. You are controlled by the Spirit if you have the Spirit of God living in you. (And remember that those who do not have the Spirit of Christ living in them do not belong to him at all.) [10] And Christ lives within you, so even though your body will die because of sin, the Spirit gives you life because you have been made right with God. [11] The Spirit of God, who raised Jesus from the dead, lives in you. And just as God raised Christ Jesus from the dead, he will give life to your mortal bodies by this same Spirit living within you."

Did you see that? Condemnation — guilt — shame — fear of not being completely free from the effects of sin — cannot co-exist in a born-again child of God. It has no those lies the devil had been telling me had no legal right to the New Creation I had become in Christ.

In fact, 2 Corinthians 5:17-21 (TLB) promises us, "[17] When someone becomes a Christian, he becomes a brand new person inside. He is not the same anymore. A new life has begun! [18] All these new things are from God who brought us back to himself through what Christ Jesus did. And God has given us the privilege of urging everyone to come into his favor and be reconciled to him. [19] For God was in Christ, restoring the world to himself, no longer counting men's sins against them but blotting them out. This is the wonderful message he has given us to tell others. [20] We are Christ's ambassadors. God is using us to speak to you: we beg you, as though Christ himself were here pleading with you, receive the love he offers you — be reconciled to God. [21] For God took the sinless Christ and poured into him our sins. Then, in exchange, he poured God's goodness into us!"

These two passages became my new anthem — I no longer had to feel guilty for my past — Jesus died to free me from that past life and to restore me to righteousness IN HIM. Though Satan continued to remind me about the things of my past, God was trying to get me to forget my past and look to my future in Him.

Though Satan was trying to convince me that I was disqualified from ministry because of my past, God was desperately calling me to Jesus and showing me all that my salvation in Christ had made available to me — including the ability and right to tell others of His great love for them too.

Not only had I been delivered from the pit of Hell, but I was "**MADE** the RIGHTEOUSNESS of GOD **IN CHRIST!**" The "old Mike" had died the day I surrendered my life to Jesus and allowed Him to carry the burdens I had been trying to carry for years.

The Mike who had done all of those horrible things years ago, no longer existed, and a brand new Mike had been born with a clean slate because of Jesus' substitutional sacrifice.

From that moment on, every time the devil would try to bring up my past, I had to remember that he wasn't talking about me — he was talking about a guy who had died many years before.

We need to learn to be like the Apostle Paul each time the devil comes to us with accusations about our pasts and declare he same truth that he declared about himself in 2 Corinthians 7:2 when he said, "Open your hearts to us. We have wronged no one, we have corrupted no one, we have cheated no one."

You see, Paul fully comprehended the work of the Cross of Jesus. He understood that He was a new creation In Christ Jesus, who had been <u>MADE</u> THE RIGHTEOUSNESS OF GOD. This wasn't anything that he had earned on his own, but something he had received freely as a joint-heir with Jesus.

I encourage you to embrace the love of God today and to cast away all of the lies that the enemy is telling you about your past. Nothing you have ever done can keep God from loving you like He does! He loves you just as much as He does Jesus—more than you could ever imagine. And there is no devil in Hell that could ever bring enough charges against you to keep God from forgiving you of everything you've done.

Begin to recognize and accept God's immeasurable LOVE, GRACE, and WILL for you to come home to Him and begin living the plan He has for you. It's a plan filled with His superabundant, more than enough, too much BLESSINGS.

There is nothing, and I mean nothing, that can separate you from His LOVE except your willful choice to reject Jesus as your Lord and Savior. GOD IS FOR YOU! So get rid of that old baggage of shame, guilt, and fear and receive all the LOVE and FAVOR God is waiting to lavish upon you once you come home and receive everything He's already made available to you in Jesus!

Daily Declaration

I am the righteousness of God in Christ! I declare that my past is behind me and the old person I once was, is dead, buried, and raised to new life in Christ. I am a totally NEW CREATION [a new species of being]. I have been redeemed from my past sins because of Jesus. Christ has become my substitutionary sacrifice — He died in my place and fully paid the price for my sins so that I don't have. I receive the pardon and freedom which Jesus has made available to me by faith. And I purpose to renew my mind to the truth that God loves me as much as he does Jesus. There is NOTHING in my past, present, or future that will ever separate me from the love of God! Thank You Father for loving me enough to send Your very best — Jesus. I receive Him and all You have made available to me as a son/daughter of Your Love. I pray all these things in the mighty name of Jesus!

Day 5
You Can't Unscramble Eggs: So Let Go Of Your Emotional Wounds

"David was greatly distressed, for the men spoke of stoning him because the souls of them all were bitterly grieved, each man for his sons and daughters. But David encouraged and strengthened himself in the Lord his God."

1 Samuel 30:6 (AMP)

One of the greatest tragedies a person can experience is to spend their lives carrying around emotional wounds and unforgiveness. Doing so robs them of their joy, their peace, and their purpose. When we focus on past hurts or wrongs that others have caused us, we deny ourselves the right to walk in the freedom of new hope for a brighter future and allow the past to steal our present and even our future.

I am not suggesting that those emotional wounds are insignificant, but the Bible tells us that there is a time to mourn and a time to rejoice.

"To everything there is a season, and a time for every matter or purpose under heaven: ² A time to be born and a time to die, a time to plant and a time to pluck up what is planted, ³ A time to kill and a time to heal, a time to break down and a time to build up, ⁴ A time to weep and a time to laugh, a time to mourn and a time to dance." (Ecclesiastes 3:1-

4).

Too many people are allowing the enemy to rob them of everything they were born and called to do, because they remained focused on the past instead of flourishing in the present. As a result, their marriages begin to suffer. Words that were spoken 20 years earlier keep them in bondage to fear, strife, and unforgiveness.

Their families suffer because they have decided to lock themselves up and refuse to allow themselves to live and enjoy life with those who matter most. In essence, they become self-made prisoners and martyrs allowing past experiences to rule their present and to determine their future.

In Isaiah 43:18-19 God says, "[18] Do not remember the former things, nor consider the things of old. [19] Behold, I will do a new thing, now it shall spring forth; shall you not know it? I will even make a road in the wilderness and rivers in the desert."

In other words, while God is trying to bring healing to those past experiences, while He is trying to restore those things that the enemy has stolen from us, and while He is working to correct the wrongs that were done—many have become so blinded by their unforgiveness and pain, that they refuse to see the "NEW THING" that God is trying to Bless them with. That's the problem with unforgiveness—it robs us of our ability to live and receive anything new.

Someone once said, "Unforgiveness is like drinking poison and expecting the other person to die." How ridiculous is that? It's crazy! But when we refuse to forgive, no matter the reason, the only people it truly hurts are ourselves and those who love us the most.

Proverbs 17:22 (ERV) tells us, "Happiness is good medicine, but sorrow is a disease." The Living Bible explains it this way, "A cheerful heart does good like medicine, but a broken spirit makes one sick." And finally, the New King James Version declares, "A merry heart does good, like medicine, but a broken spirit dries the bones."

Dr. David Levy a leading neurosurgeon and medical professor at UCSD says, "Bitterness is contrary to cheerfulness and is characterized by anger, hostility, antagonism, fear, anxiety, distress, with the list going on and on. It dries up our very bones. Our immune system is manufactured in the marrow of our bones. Research has proven unforgiveness as one cause for disease in our bodies. There are many reasons to forgive."

Catherine Ponder writes, "When you hold resentment towards another, you are bound to that person or condition by an emotional link that is stronger than steel. Forgiveness is the ONLY way to dissolve that link and get FREE."

In 1 Samuel 30, David and his men are fighting against the Amalekites. They have left their women and children behind at home and have gone away to war. Yet while they are away, a band of Amalekites go into their village, burn their city to the ground, and take all of the women and children away as captives.

When the Israelites return from war the men are furious with David. They blame him for their misery and plot to kill him. Their families have been taken and they have no hope of ever seeing them again.

Another way of looking at this is: these Israelite warriors have become overwhelmed by the grief and pain of losing their families. They have become so distraught that they have allowed the pain of their loss to steal their dreams of ever enjoying life again. They were attacked; hurt by others, and they can't find the courage to move forward in hope for anything but their present pain and emotional wounds.

The part of this story that we need to pay special attention to, are the last eleven words of verse 6. The Amplified Bible says, ***"But David encouraged and strengthened himself in the Lord his God."*** (Emphasis Added).

David had just lost everything. He lost both of his wives to the Amalekite bandits. His friends and family wanted to kill him for something he hadn't caused. He had no guarantee in the natural that his life would ever return to joy. He didn't even know if he would make it through the day. But the Bible says that he encouraged and strengthened himself in the Lord.

We must remember that God is at His strongest when we are at our weakest! If we will muster up the faith to turn to God and to place our faith in Him to bring us through our storm — He will.

We may not "feel" like praising God when we've been hurt, but as Christians, we are not moved by our feelings — but by our faith (See 2 Corinthians 5:7). Praise is a powerful spiritual weapon which ushers in the presence and power of the Lord and gets Him moving and operating on our behalf.

Isaiah 43:29 (AMP) promises us, "He gives power to the faint and weary, and to him who has no might He increases strength [causing it to multiply and making it to abound]."

Philippians 4:13 (AMP) declares, "I have strength for all things in Christ Who empowers me [I am ready for anything and equal to anything through Him Who infuses inner strength into me; I am self-sufficient in Christ's sufficiency]."

And Nehemiah 8:10 (NLT) Commands us, "Don't be dejected and sad, for the joy of the LORD is your strength!"

We must all understand that it's impossible to unscramble eggs. In other words, we cannot change the things that have already happened, but we can choose to forgive ourselves and to forgive those who have wronged us. We can determine to either move forward in love and in faith trusting God to work out and heal the wounds we've experienced or we can remain stuck and poison ourselves and our loved ones.

We could conceivably spend the rest of our lives asking questions like "Why me?" "How come?" or "What could I have done differently?" But that won't change those circumstances.

Instead of spending our lives allowing those past hurts to determine our future, why don't we do as the Apostle Paul did, and begin saying, "[13] No, dear brothers and sisters, I have not achieved it, but I focus on this one thing: Forgetting the past and looking forward to what lies ahead, [14] I press on to reach the end of the race and receive the heavenly prize for which God, through Christ Jesus, is calling us." (See Philippians 3:13-14, NLT).

Ephesians 4:31-32 (NLT) tells us to, "[31] Get rid of all bitterness, rage, anger, harsh words, and slander, as well as all types of evil behavior. [32] Instead, be kind to each other, tenderhearted, forgiving one another, just as God through Christ has forgiven you."

Notice what Jesus said about unforgiveness. In Matthew 6:14-15, "[14] For if you forgive men their trespasses, your heavenly Father will also forgive you. [15] But if you do not forgive men their trespasses, neither will your Father forgive your trespasses."

In Mark 11:25 Jesus said almost the exact same thing, "And whenever you stand praying, if you have anything against anyone, forgive him, that your Father in heaven may also forgive you your trespasses." Forgiveness is not an option—it's a COMMAND for every follower of Jesus!

I encourage you today to get into the Word of God and then go to the Throne of Grace and allow yourself to forgive and to release those past hurts that others have caused you. Don't allow the enemy to rob you of your present or your future. Don't allow your unforgiveness to stop-up the river of God's favor and Blessing.

God wants to bring you healing in every area of your life, but in order for Him to give it to you—YOU MUST release the past hurts and wounds others have caused you and receive what God is offering to you in return—Beauty for your ashes, Healing for your wounds, and Hope for your future!

Let go of your emotional wounds, begin to encourage and to strengthen yourself in the Lord, and receive God's healing, His restoration, and His Blessing in your life today! He loves you—can you receive His love and move forward in faith?

Daily Declaration

Today I choose to forgive and to release everyone who has wounded me physically, emotionally, mentally, and spiritually. I refuse to poison myself with the bitterness of unforgiveness. I declare that the responsibility to correct and heal me of the wounds that I have received from others is the Lord's, because I have cast my cares upon Him. I will not be moved by the tactics of the devil, but I will only be moved by my faith in God and His Word! I am more than a conqueror in Christ. I am the head and not the tail! The joy of the Lord is my strength and I will praise God in the midst of my pain. The Bible tells me that God is for me and if He is for me who dare stand against me? I declare that I choose to walk in love even with those who wish to hurt me. The battle is the Lord's and the VICTORY is mine — because I choose God and I choose LOVE! I pray these things in Jesus' name, Amen.

Day 6
Let God Rule In Your Heart And Your Mind

"Let God be true but every man a liar. As it is written: That you may be justified in your words, and may overcome when you are judged."

Romans 3:4

I am constantly amazed by the society in which we live. There are arguments for everything under the sun even in Christians circles, regarding how we should vote, the things that we stand for and oppose, we even argue over which parts of the Bible we believe and which parts we don't! If any group should have things together and be walking in love, you would think that Christians should — but that's often not the case.

Why not? Because political correctness better known as Luke-warm Christianity has crept into the Church and begun to corrupt the minds and actions of even God's elite.

It's absolutely appalling when mainstream Christian denominations begin embracing things like mixing Christianity and Islam together [Chrislam]. Or when pastors move away from teaching and believing the basic tenants of the Christian faith such as: the virgin birth, the death, burial, and resurrection of Christ, the belief that faith in Jesus is the ONLY way to receive salvation, etc.

Some denominations have even started allowing homosexual ministers to lead their congregations and perform homosexual marriages sanctioned by the church, when the Bible explicitly opposes all of these sins.

In a day when everybody has their own philosophy and standard for determining right from wrong based on personal experience and ideology, how do we decide who's right and how we should live our lives?

In a time when one "Christian" berates another calling him/her a "bigot" and refuting their stand on the teachings of the Bible, because that person rejects the popular worldviews and acts of compromise to please men instead of pleasing over God—how do we continue to standing for THE TRUTH?

I suggest that the **_ONLY WAY_** is by choosing to allow the Bible to frame not only our beliefs about right and wrong, but also allow it to direct our thinking, our words, and our actions.

There is a standard which surpasses all others, and that standard is the Word of God. I know what you're thinking: _But what about those people who don't believe the Bible?_ It is still the standard by which every one of us will be judged whether we believe it or not!

Just because I may not believe that driving 120 miles per hour on the interstate is dangerous, there is still a penalty for doing—my personal philosophy doesn't change the law of the land.

The same is true when we're talking about healing, miracles, the Holy Spirit, the power of our words, prophecy, etc. Many people want to argue about whether those things are "still for today or whether they have passed away," based on their personal experiences or traditions, but the Bible easily settles the argument if we allow it to.

Hebrews 13:8 states, "Jesus Christ is the same yesterday, today, and forever."

That said, we must ask ourselves the questions, "Did Jesus or anyone else ever heal the sick, prophesy, speak in tongues, receive the Holy Spirit, hear the voice of God, witness miracles." Yes, of course! Well then, if God hasn't changed, then these things are still available whether we ever experience them personally or not! If we want to experience these things we must study the Bible and apply it's teachings to our lives.

Philippians 4:6-9, tells us that no matter what it is we desire, if we want our prayers to be answered we must follow God's method in order to receive His promises. "6 Be anxious for nothing, but in everything by prayer and supplication, with thanksgiving, let your requests be made known to God; 7 and the peace of God, which surpasses all understanding, will guard your hearts and minds through Christ Jesus. 8 Finally, brethren, whatever things are true, whatever things are noble, whatever things are just, whatever things are pure, whatever things are lovely, whatever things are of good report, if there is any virtue and if there is anything praiseworthy – meditate on these things. 9 The things which you learned and received and heard and saw in me, these do, and the God of peace will be with you."

That is one of the standards for receiving answered prayer, another is found in Mark 11:22-24 (NKJV) which declares, "22 So Jesus answered and said to them, "Have faith in God. 23 For assuredly, I say to you, whoever says to this mountain, 'Be removed and be cast into the sea,' and does not

STANDING BETWEEN YOUR AMEN & HALLELUJAH

doubt in his heart, but believes that those things he says will be done, he will have whatever he says. [24] Therefore I say to you, whatever things you ask when you pray, believe that you receive them, and you will have them." What's the requirement for answered prayer according to these words Jesus spoke to His disciples? Faith in God and confidence in what you have said based on what He's already promised you could have IN CHRIST.

I've said all of this to encourage you not to be dissuaded in your faith by anyone whether they be a pastor, a friend, a family member or a non-believing professor at your college.

Take Romans 3:4 to heart and allow the Bible to be the STANDARD for your life. Allow the TRUTH of the Word to guide your words, your thinking, your actions, and your life. Make Romans 3:4 your life's motto, "Let God be true but every man a liar. As it is written: 'That you may be justified in your words, and may overcome when you are judged.'"

When you choose to live on the God side of life, you are ALWAYS VICTORIOUS — PRAISE JESUS!!!

Daily Declaration

I declare that the Bible is the STANDARD for my life. I refuse to bow down to political correctness, to pressures of others, and to flat-out compromise. God is my Source in everything. Apart from Him I am powerless and unfruitful. Holy Spirit I ask you for your wisdom and help during these troubling times. Help me to live a holy life that God will be proud of. Lead me and guide me into all truth and protect me from the traps that the devil has set to trip me up and try to make me fall away from Your TRUTH. Father, I give myself completely to You. I surrender my will to Yours. I love You more than life itself and I am Blessed when You speak to me and shower me with Your goodness. You are a Good God! I am grateful to have You in my life. Thank You, Thank You, Thank You for never leaving me or forsaking me. I BLESS You with my whole spirit, soul, mind, and strength, and I pray these things in Jesus' name, Amen!

Day 7
Have You Given Your Angels An Assignment?

"¹³ But to which of the angels has He ever said: "Sit at My right hand, till I make Your enemies Your footstool"? ¹⁴ Are they not all ministering spirits sent forth to minister for those who will inherit salvation?"

Hebrews 1:13-14

Did you know that you have angelic help assigned to you? You do! The Bible tells us that angels are all ministering spirits sent by God, to minister for those who will inherit salvation. If you have received Jesus as your personal Lord and Savior—then that includes YOU!

Romans 10:8-10 says, "⁸ But what does it say? "The word is near you, in your mouth and in your heart" (that is, the word of faith which we preach): ⁹ that if you confess with your mouth the Lord Jesus and believe in your heart that God has raised Him from the dead, you will be saved. ¹⁰ For with the heart one believes unto righteousness, and with the mouth confession is made unto salvation."

Confessing Jesus as Lord, immediately changed your life in many ways. You not only changed your eternal spiritual destination, you not only gained access to the promises of God found in His Word, but you also gained a huge spiritual arsenal of help, to assist you in your day to day dealings. This arsenal includes angelic hosts, who not only listen to God's commands, but also to yours.

In Daniel chapter 10, we get a glimpse into how powerful the words and prayers of a believer truly are. In verse 12, the angel Gabriel appears to Daniel and says to him, "Do not fear, Daniel, for from the first day that you set your heart to understand, and to humble yourself before your God, *your words were heard; and I have come because of your words.*" (Emphasis Added).

Did you read that carefully? The angel came because of Daniels WORDS of prayer! That is exciting, amazing, and awesome! The angel Gabriel was sent on assignment to help Daniel, because of his humility to the promises of God and because he humbled and aligned his words with the Word of God.

The Bible tells us that the angel Gabriel came to answer Daniel's prayer and to give him insight into why it had taken twenty one days for the answer to take place.

Gabriel then explains to Daniel, "But the prince of the kingdom of Persia [Satan] withstood me twenty-one days; and behold, Michael [the Archangel], one of the chief princes, came to help me, (Daniel 10:13).

Satan's forces were trying everything they could to hinder Daniel's prayers from coming to pass, but they couldn't stop it from becoming a reality. In all of their attempts, they could only delay it slightly, hoping that Daniel would give up, become discouraged, and begin complaining against God.

This should make you SHOUT! The enemy doesn't have the ability to stop the Word the goes out of your mouth! He doesn't have the ability to defeat you or cancel out your prayers unless you allow him to steal them by becoming double-minded.

So stick with the Word, remain faithful, trusting God to do what He promised, and give your angels an assignment by releasing your faith and prayers into the atmosphere. You may one day hear the same words Daniel heard...I have come because of your words!

Daily Declaration

Angels, Go now and bring in my harvest in Jesus mighty name! I charge you to do whatever it takes to stop the attempts of the enemy against me and to bring the Blessing which my Heavenly Father has commanded upon me – The BLESSING IS MINE NOW! Deuteronomy 28:1-14 (MSG) declares of me: [1-6] If you listen obediently to the Voice of GOD, your God, and heartily obey all his commandments that I command you today, GOD, your God, will place you on high, high above all the nations of the world. All these blessings will come down on you and spread out beyond you because you have responded to the Voice of GOD, your God: GOD's blessing inside the city, GOD's blessing in the country; GOD's blessing on your children, the crops of your land, the young of your livestock, the calves of your herds, the lambs of your flocks. GOD's blessing on your basket and bread bowl; GOD's blessing in your coming in, GOD's blessing in your going out. [7] GOD will defeat your enemies who attack you. They'll come at you on one road and run away on seven roads. [8] GOD will order a blessing on your barns and workplaces; he'll bless you in the land that GOD, your God, is giving you. [9] GOD will form you as a people holy to him, just as he promised you, if you keep the commandments of GOD, your God, and live the way he has shown you. [10] All the peoples on Earth will see you living under the Name of GOD and hold you in respectful awe. [11-14] GOD will lavish you with good things: children from your womb, offspring from your animals, and crops from your land, the land that GOD promised your ancestors that he would give you. GOD will throw open the doors of his sky vaults and pour rain on your land on schedule and bless the work you take in hand. You will lend to many nations but you yourself won't have to take out a loan. GOD will make you the head, not the tail; you'll always be the top dog, never the bottom dog, as you obediently listen to and diligently keep the commands of GOD, your God, that I am commanding you today. Don't swerve an inch to the right or left from the words that I command you today by going off following and worshiping other gods."

If that is what God has promised me then that is what I shall have! I choose to walk in obedience to His commands and His plans for my life. I humble myself before His mighty hand and I receive His BLESSING on every area of my life. Angels—Go Now! I send you on assignment! Bring in my harvest—in the mighty name of Jesus, Amen.

Day 8
Covenant Wealth

"And you shall remember the LORD your God, for it is He who
gives you power to get wealth, that He may establish His
covenant which He swore to your fathers, as it is this day."

Deuteronomy 8:18

Did you know that covenant is the most powerful
agreement that exists in this world? The Word
covenant is translated from the Hebrew word *Brit*,
which means: to cut where blood flows.

The idea behind covenant is an unbreakable vow or
agreement made between two parties. This agreement is so
binding between the two making covenant, that if one breaks
the agreement, the penalty for doing so is death.

Each party is also bound to share all they have with the
other, in order to help sustain them and bless them — even to
point of sacrificing their own life for the other.

Throughout the world when groups would come
together to cut the covenant, a weaker party would submit to
a stronger and agree to be bound to the other in exchange for
protection, help, etc.

If one covenant partner has something that the other
needs, that thing will be freely provided, in order to honor the
covenant agreement which was made.

For example: let's say that there is a tribe of farmers
and a tribe of warriors who cut a covenant with one another.
The farming tribe has plenty of food, but other predatory

tribes who aren't as skilled in farming come in and steal their crops and kill their families. This occurs because even though the farming tribe is proficient in growing crops, they are weak when it comes down to protecting themselves against predatory tribes. As a result this farming tribe decides to cut a covenant with a warrior tribe in exchange for access to their bountiful crops.

The warrior tribe agrees because even though they are fierce warriors, they are dying off because they cannot feed themselves adequately. When these two tribes come together, both benefit from the other's strengths. The weaker farming tribe now has protection and the warrior tribe has the food it needs to remain strong and healthy.

The same is true with God and His children. God wanted a family, so He created and made a covenant with man to establish His Kingdom in the earth. God found a man named Abram whom He could depend on and He covenanted with him and promised to care for and supply all of Abram's needs if he would obey and follow God.

Through this covenant, God then made all He had available to Abram—whom He later re-named Abraham. God gave him wealth, flocks, lands, servants, good health in old age, and most importantly a son through which the Messiah would come and save the entire world.

Abraham, unlike most Christians today, knew who his source was. He depended on God to supply all of his needs and He honored God with all that he owned. If he had it, he knew it was only because of God's goodness. If God asked for it, Abraham was willing to give it up knowing that God would give it back.

That is why Abraham could say to his servants who traveled with him when he went to offer Isaac as a sacrifice in Genesis 22:5 (NLT), "[5] Stay here with the donkey, the boy and I will travel a little farther. We will worship there, and then we will come right back."

Even though God asked Abraham to offer his covenant heir as a sacrificial offering, he knew how powerfully important covenant was to God.

He knew that if God had promised to bring Abraham's descendants through Isaac, He would have to somehow miraculously raise him back up from the dead, or risk breaking His covenant vow. It wouldn't be "good enough," to simply give him another son, it had to be Isaac — because Isaac was the covenanted heir from his own flesh through which God had promised to give all of the land of Canaan. (See Genesis 15).

Hebrews 11:17 (NLT) says, "It was by faith that Abraham offered Isaac as a sacrifice when God was testing him. Abraham, who had received God's promises, was ready to sacrifice his only son, Isaac."

Abraham had a binding contract with God. He knew that God could do the impossible, because he had witnessed it over and over. So even though there must have been some anxiety and symptoms of trepidation, Abraham obeyed trusting that God would do all He had promised.

What has God asked you to do that has caused you some trepidation, anxiety, maybe even doubt? God has made a strong and sacred agreement to take care of you and to be your God. There is **NOTHING** that is too hard for Him to accomplish through you, in you, or around you.

The decision is now in your court. Are you going to remain right where you are, holding back, cowering in fear, and listening to the devil tell you that if you do _____, you'll never see _____.

That didn't stop Abraham because he knew that it was impossible for God to lie or break His covenant. Abraham knew that God's name was on the line. I encourage you to be bold like our father Abraham. Trust God, believe the promises in the Word, and step out in faith believing to receive the fulfillment of the promise and vision God has placed inside of you. It's a covenant thing!

Daily Declaration

Father, I trust You more than anything in this world. Even if everyone should abandon me, cheat me, and lie about me, I know that You will never leave me as an orphan without help in this world. In fact, John 14:15-20 (AMP) promises, "[15] If you [really] love Me, you will keep (obey) My commands. [16] And I will ask the Father, and He will give you another Comforter (Counselor, Helper, Intercessor, Advocate, Strengthener, and Standby), that He may remain with you forever — [17] The Spirit of Truth, Whom the world cannot receive (welcome, take to its heart), because it does not see Him or know *and* recognize Him. But you know *and* recognize Him, for He lives with you [constantly] and will be in you. [18] I will not leave you as orphans [comfortless, desolate, bereaved, forlorn, helpless]; I will come [back] to you. [19] Just a little while now, and the world will not see Me anymore, but you will see Me; because I live, you will live also. [20] At that time [when that day comes] you will know [for yourselves] that I am in My Father, and you [are] in Me, and I [am] in you." Lord, I trust you. I know that You are a covenant keeping God. I understand that Your holy Word is compete TRUTH and I put my life into Your care. Thank You for loving me. I love You and thank You for Your Son Jesus! I pray these things in Jesus' name, Amen.

Day 9
Confidence In Prayer

"^{14} Now this is the confidence that we have in Him, that if we ask anything according to His will, He hears us. ^{15} And if we know that He hears us, whatever we ask, we know that we have the petitions that we have asked of Him."

1 John 5:14-15

How important is confidence? Many would argue that confidence is KEY when it concerns matters of FAITH. For example, if you were going to deposit your money in a bank, you would first want to be confident that your money would be protected in the event of a robbery, fire, or bank closure. You'd want to have the promise that your money would be replaced...That is confidence.

If you were going to purchase a $30,000.00 used car and you wanted to make sure that it would last after you bought it, you would most likely take it to a mechanic to verify its condition.

Once you'd received the green light from the mechanic, you would then have the confidence you were making a "good purchase." Without confidence—you cannot have any sense of surety or guarantee! And according to the Bible, if you don't remain steadfast in your faith—YOU HAVE NO RIGHT TO EXPECT ANYTHING FROM GOD!

"[6] But let him ask in faith, nothing wavering. For he that wavereth is like a wave of the sea driven with the wind and tossed.[7] For let not that man think that he shall receive any thing of the Lord.[8] A double minded man is unstable in all his ways." (James 1:6-8, KJV).

The same is true with any promise. If I have never promised you anything, you have no right to expect anything from me. However, if I've promised to buy you a new suit or dress after church this Sunday, then you have my word—my commitment to follow through with whatever I have promised.

In fact, that promise is specific—it is detailed. What if I promised that I would buy you a suit or dress after church this Sunday—If you washed my car? Then, there would be a condition that would have to be met in order to receive my promise.

The Bible is chock-full of promises which God has made to his Children and 99% if not all of them are conditional.

The main condition to receiving any promise from God's Word is dependent on whether or not you receive Jesus as your personal Lord and Savior. If Jesus is not YOUR Lord, then YOU have NO RIGHT to HIS COVENANT PROMISES.

Galatians 3:29 tells us, "And if you are Christ's, then you are Abraham's seed, and heirs according to the promise." What Promise is Paul talking about here in this passage? The same covenant promise or promises that God made to Abraham in Genesis 15 and in Deuteronomy 28—The Promise of THE BLESSING! Hallelujah!

And Proverbs 10:22 (AMP) declares, "The blessing of the Lord — it makes [truly] rich, and He adds no sorrow with it [neither does toiling increase it].

In other words, The Blessing of God causes each and every area of your life to become better. Yet, it begins in your spirit — freeing you from the Curse and changing your eternal destination. But don't try to limit God's Blessing — it also heals and improves your relationships with others, your health, it restores those things the enemy has stolen from you, and blesses you physically, mentally, soulishly, and even materially — which also includes your finances.

Secondly, God expects you to have faith or confident trust that He will honor and do exactly what He has promised you in the Bible. Your responsibility is to get in the Word and discover those promises for yourself and then make sure that you are meeting the conditions to receive them.

Isaiah 1:19 states, "If you are willing and obedient, you shall eat the good of the land." What's the promise God has made in this verse? He has promised that YOU will eat or enjoy the good of the land — have success, enjoying prosperity, and have sufficient supply, etc. But there is a condition to this promise. The condition stipulates that YOU MUST BE WILLING AND OBEDIENT to God's commands.

Someone might say, "Well that's just ridiculous, who wouldn't want to be successful, have sufficient supply, etc.?" That's simple, someone who craves pity, and enjoys whining about their problems to others instead of enjoying self-sufficiency and humbling themselves before God.

If you want to have your prayers answered, you need to make sure that they are based on the Word of God. You MUST become confident in the fact that when you pray in line with Scripture, God will hear your prayers. And because He hears, He will actively bring them to pass because He has a covenant agreement with you, and because You obey His commands.

You must become confident that because God made those promises to you, He is not only capable of bringing them to pass, but He is also willing to give them to you because He loves you.

Once that important issue has been settled, the only things left to do is to believe Him, and to thank Him for your answer until it shows up.

If I was to give you a great gift, the first thing out of your mouth should be THANK YOU. Well, faith believes the promises of God and gives Him praise and thanksgiving for those gifts, even before they show up in the natural. Thank You Jesus! I believe I receive—It's MINE! In Jesus' name.

Daily Declaration

I declare that I am a believer, not a doubter. I have world overcoming faith and confidence in my God. My God is faithful, just, loving, merciful, and gracious. I am Blessed whether I ever receive another gift from God or not. I believe for the impossible and I receive the inconceivable. The supernatural is the ordinary in my life. Thank You Father for all of the things you have done, are doing, and will do in my life! I declare that I am a magnet to Your Blessing. Just as Psalm 23:6 (MSG) declares, "Your beauty and love chase after me every day of my life." You overwhelm me with Your goodness Lord! I am Blessed beyond measure. I live in the richness of your unmerited favor because You go before me and behind me and encompass me like a shield (See Psalm 5:12). Thank You Jesus for all that You do! I pray these things in the mighty name of Jesus, Amen.

Day 10
Never Run At Your Giant With Your Mouth Shut

"⁴³ So the Philistine said to David, "Am I a dog that you come to me with sticks?" And the Philistine cursed David by his gods. ⁴⁴ And the Philistine said to David, "Come to me, and I will give your flesh to the birds of the air and the beasts of the field!" ⁴⁵ Then David said to the Philistine, "You come to me with a sword, with a spear, and with a javelin. But I come to you in the name of the LORD of hosts, the God of the armies of Israel, whom you have defied. ⁴⁶ This day the LORD will deliver you into my hand, and I will strike you and take your head from you. And this day I will give the carcasses of the camp of the Philistines to the birds of the air and the wild beasts of the earth, that all the earth may know that there is a God in Israel. ⁴⁷ Then all this assembly shall know that the LORD does not save with sword and spear; for the battle *is* the LORD's, and He will give you into our hands."

1 Samuel 17:43-47

Have you ever noticed that the enemy is always talking to you, trying to get your attention, and trying to shake your confidence? In California where I grew up, that is called "TALKING SMACK."

As a kid, I played many sports, but my two favorites were baseball and wrestling. In both of these sports, my opponent would often make noises or talk smack, trying to get me off my game. Whether it was, "Aye batter batter, swing," or a literal taunt about taking me out on the mat, both were geared to try to get me to feel defeated even before I got onto the field or got to the mat.

The devil works the same way. He will talk smack to you, trying to distract you and get you to walk in defeat by suggesting thoughts or by placing negative images in your mind. He will also try to convince you to accept sickness and disease by placing symptoms in your body, but you don't have to receive them! You have been redeemed from the CURSE — Hallelujah!

Satan understands that if he can cause you to be moved by these things, then he will win the battle. If can get you to receive and react to them by saying things like, *Well, its flu season, I guess it's just our turn to be sick*, then he will turn up the pressure.

But as I mentioned before, we don't have to put up with that junk! The Bible tells us that when the devil brings his symptoms to us our responsibility is, "⁵Casting down imaginations, and every high thing that exalteth itself against the knowledge of God, and bringing into captivity every thought to the obedience of Christ." (2 Corinthians 10:5, KJV).

When the enemy TALKS SMACK, and tells you that you have to yield to sickness, that you have to receive poverty, or that he's going to take you out of this life — that's when you need to do what David did and shut his mouth by talking back to him.

I just love David's boldness as he talks back to Goliath who has called him out and has threatened to kill him, the Bible says, "⁴¹⁻⁴² As the Philistine paced back and forth, his shield bearer in front of him, he noticed David. He took one look down on him and sneered — a mere youngster, apple-cheeked and peach-fuzzed. [43] The Philistine ridiculed David. "Am I a dog that you come after me with a stick?" And he cursed him by his gods. [44] "Come on," said the Philistine. "I'll make roadkill of you for the buzzards. I'll turn you into a tasty morsel for the field mice." [45-47] *David answered,* "You come at me with sword and spear and battle-ax. I come at you in the name of GOD-of-the-Angel-Armies, the God of Israel's troops, whom you curse and mock. This very day GOD is handing you over to me. *I'm about to kill you, cut off your head, and serve up your body and the bodies of your Philistine buddies to the crows and coyotes. The whole earth will know that there's an extraordinary God in Israel. And everyone gathered here will learn that GOD doesn't save by means of sword or spear. The battle belongs to GOD — he's handing you to us on a platter!"* (1 Samuel 17:41-47, MSG — Emphasis Added).

Don't sit there feeling sorry for yourself, listening to him as he continues to make threats. Begin talking back. Open up your mouth and speak the Word! Tell him what Jesus has done for you. Tell him how Christ has delivered you from the Curse through His the blood. And then reminded him how he's already been defeated by your big brother Jesus. Remind him that the Bibles says, that Jesus beat him so badly that He made a show of him (Colossians 2:15).

Learn to drown out the devil's voice with words of faith! Speak the promises of Blessing over your life. Contradict every thought of doubt that he tries to convince you to receive and run him away with the Word.

It's your choice. You're in control. And you have all the weapons necessary to run him off. Don't take smack from that defeated pipsqueak, run at him with the Word of God in your mouth, with the Name of Jesus, and remind him of THE BLOOD. Send him scrambling for cover with his tail tucked between his legs.

Remind him that he's been defeated and that he's not allowed anywhere near your family, your finances, your business, your relationships, your health, etc. Remind him that you have NO TRESPASSING signs posted all over your property and that the penalty for trespassing is the full extent of the Word! YOU'VE GOT THE VICTORY IN JESUS!

Daily Declaration

I declare that I am a mighty man/woman of valor. No demon in Hell has authority over me because I have been redeemed by the BLOOD of Jesus! I am BLOOD bought and set FREE from the Curse of the Law—because Jesus took my place—dying so that I would be FREE. (See Isaiah 53:4-5, Galatians 3:13-14, 1 Peter 2:24). Satan, I bind you in the name of Jesus! You take your hands off of God's property. I am His and He is mine. I plead the BLOOD of Jesus over myself, over my family, and over everything that belongs to me. I am drawing a line in the sand today and you better not cross it in Jesus' mighty name—or risk the consequences for doing so. Angels, I charge you to go forth and protect what is mine. Go now, bring in my harvest, protect my family, set-up opportunities for me to be Blessed and to be a Blessing to others in Jesus name. Satan, I rebuke you and cast you out in Jesus' name. I resist you and command you to flee now! I pray these things in Jesus' mighty name—the name above EVERY name which is named—AMEN.

Day 11
Humbling Yourself Before LOVE

"If My people who are called by My name will humble themselves, and pray and seek My face, and turn from their wicked ways, then I will hear from heaven, and will forgive their sin and heal their land."

2 Chronicles 7:14

We all have people in our lives that we want to see blessed, victorious, and abounding in God's supernatural favor. These include people like our family members, our children, our brothers and sisters in Christ, our pastors and their families. We want them to do better than we've done and to experience more of God's Blessing than we have up to this point. Why? Because we love them! It might be a surprise, but God feels the same about YOU!

Our God is a GOOD GOD. In 1 John 4:8-11; 14-16, He has said of Himself — that HE IS LOVE. "[8] He who does not love does not know God, for God is love. [9] In this the love of God was manifested toward us, that God has sent His only begotten Son into the world, that we might live through Him. [10] In this is love, not that we loved God, but that He loved us and sent His Son *to be* the propitiation [full payment] for our sins. [11] Beloved, if God so loved us, we also ought to love one another...[14] And we have seen and testify that the Father has sent the Son *as* Savior of the world. [15] Whoever confesses that Jesus is the Son of God, God abides in him, and he in God. [16] And we have known and believed the love that God has for us. God is love, and he who abides in love abides in God, and God in him."

Because of God loves us so—He sent Jesus to completely restore us back to what we were before sin entered the earth through Adam and Eve.

In 2 Chronicles 7:14, God promises, "If my people who are called by my name will humble themselves…"

The original Hebrew says, "Then my people will humble or bow before me, those whom I have begged and urged to myself and named my people."

Wait, I'm confused? I thought it said, "If my people…" Where did the "Then" come from? Earlier in the same chapter Solomon made an enormous sacrifice and God was pleased. God then calls the temple Solomon has dedicated as His house of sacrifice.

God is pleased, but He knows that His people are flawed and unfaithful. One day they're obedient and follow after Him, the next, they reject His ways and act like animals.

In this passage God is saying, "I know that you're going to blow it again, I have given you a free will to choose between right and wrong. I have even given you the opportunity to reject me altogether. When you do reject Me and My ways, the enemy naturally rushes in and creates destruction, disorder, and death. But because of My GREAT LOVE FOR YOU, I have made a way to bring you back to wholeness, complete restoration, perfect peace and security. I will do this "If," you will turn back to Me and receive My love. "If," you will humble yourselves and honor My commands. "If," you will be faithful and honor Me as your God. I will then, pour out My love, My healing, My grace, and My covenant goodness all over you. The choice is yours. (See Deuteronomy 30:19).

God then says, "and [they will] pray and seek My face, and turn from their wicked ways, then I will hear from heaven."

The Hebrew words that are translated as *seek* and *face* literally mean to desire or to crave God's presence, His goodness. Once you have lived in the BLESSING of God you don't want to return to the world's garbage. You crave the things of God more than you do the façade of the world.

I like what Jesse Duplantis says, "I've been broke and I've been rich...I like rich better." That is so true with God, once you have tasted His goodness, nothing else compares. In fact, David explained it this way, "Oh, taste and see that the LORD is good; Blessed is the man who trusts in Him!"

Once Man returns to God and begins to crave and desire His goodness and His love for them, He says, "Then I will hear from heaven, and will forgive their sin and heal their land."

The word that is translated as *hear*, means to listen, to hear, to be attentive to, to obey. In essence, God is saying, "Before you chose to return to me, I didn't have the legal right to operate on your behalf.

Think of it this way: if you crash your car and call State Farm insurance company saying, "I wrecked my car and need to have it repaired." What is the first thing they are going to ask you for? YOUR POLICY NUMBER.

God is saying, "You need to choose Me, obey Me, desire Me, and by doing so, that gives you access to my covenant promises. Or in today's vernacular — it gives you access to a "heavenly policy" so to speak. It allows God to operate on your behalf. It allows Him to restore you to complete wholeness IN CHRIST JESUS!

I'm not saying that God doesn't have the ability to act, but He has limited Himself by what He has spoken in His Word the Bible. He doesn't change and He will not go against the promises made to us in the Bible. We see a prime example of this in Judges Chapter 10.

"6 Then the children of Israel again did evil in the sight of the LORD, and served the Baals and the Ashtoreths, the gods of Syria, the gods of Sidon, the gods of Moab, the gods of the people of Ammon, and the gods of the Philistines; and they forsook the LORD and did not serve Him. 7 So the anger of the LORD was hot against Israel; and He sold them into the hands of the Philistines and into the hands of the people of Ammon. 8 From that year they harassed and oppressed the children of Israel for eighteen years — all the children of Israel who were on the other side of the Jordan in the land of the Amorites, in Gilead. 9 Moreover the people of Ammon crossed over the Jordan to fight against Judah also, against Benjamin, and against the house of Ephraim, so that Israel was severely distressed. 10 And the children of Israel cried out to the LORD, saying, "We have sinned against You, because we have both forsaken our God and served the Baals!" 11 So the LORD said to the children of Israel, "Did I not deliver you from the Egyptians and from the Amorites and from the people of Ammon and from the Philistines? 12 Also the Sidonians and Amalekites and Maonites oppressed you; and you cried out to Me, and I delivered you from their hand. 13 Yet you have forsaken Me and served other gods. Therefore I will deliver you no more. 14 *"Go and cry out to the gods which you have*

chosen; let them deliver you in your time of distress."
(Emphasis Added).

Make the decision today, to desire God, to crave His goodness, and to allow Him to operate on your behalf. Humble yourself before Him and repent of your sins. Thank Him for being your great and mighty God. He loves you passionately and wants to Bless you with all of His Love—that's just who He is!

Daily Declaration

Father, I humble myself before You today and ask You to forgive me of ALL of my sins. You are My God! Your Word IS TRUTH and I submit before You and ALL that You have commanded. Thank You for protecting me, Blessing me, and Loving me beyond what I deserve. I am grateful for your unlimited mercy and overwhelming grace. Your love surpasses my human understanding, but I receive it all by faith, in Jesus' name. Holy Spirit, help me to follow after Jesus. Teach me to love like Him, to forgive like Him, to Bless others the way He Blessed, and to hear and obey the voice of the Father like He heard and obeyed. I want to be just like Jesus. I want to do the things He did and to experience the miracles that He performed. Just like the famous hymn declares, I give You all that I am and I surrender ALL to Jesus. I pray these things in Jesus' name, Amen.

Day 12
God <u>NEVER</u> Harms Us To Teach Us A Lesson

"The thief comes only in order to steal and kill and destroy. I came that they may have and enjoy life, and have it in abundance (to the full, till it overflows)."

John 10:10 (AMP)

I don't know about you, but it really irks me when people blame God for their problems. If you have received Jesus as Lord—God is not your problem—H He is your lifeline. Most of the time, God is blamed for things that we've caused. He's blamed for things that we have allowed through the words we have spoken. He is blamed for things the enemy has caused, through doors that we've opened up to him as a result of our sin.

Have you ever heard a newscaster claim that a tornado or a hurricane was an "act of God?" Have you ever heard someone say something like, "God put this cancer on me to teach me a lesson and to bring Him glory?"

God is not in the business of putting sickness and disease on people to teach them a lesson! He doesn't kill babies because He needs more angels in Heaven. And He doesn't send tornados to destroy houses just to grab our attention! He is the God of the BLESSING!

Let me ask you a question. How would sickness, death, and destruction bring God glory? God doesn't have those things in Heaven because they are all part of the CURSE. In fact, they are in stark contrast to His character? God never intended for man to die when He placed him in the Garden of Eden. Death, Sickness, and destruction all came as a result of Adam's sin and mankind's fall.

Don't misunderstand me; there's certainly a penalty for sin. Our God is a JUST JUDGE, and He requires justice. In fact the Bible clearly explains that we reap what we sow. However, when we sin, we open ourselves up to the enemy by choosing to operate in opposition to the Bible's commands (SEE Deut. 30:19), and the Curse is what we reap in return.

In Genesis 4:6-7, we find Cain mad for having his sacrifice/offering rejected by God. "[6] So the LORD said to Cain, "Why are you angry? And why has your countenance fallen? [7] If you do well, will you not be accepted? And if you do not do well, sin lies at the door. And its desire is for you, but you should rule over it."

In other words, your decision to either obey or disobey God's commands determines Satan's ability to gain access into your circumstances. God tells us that we should rule over evil, have dominion over sin, sickness, disease, poverty, bad relationships, and everything else tied to the Curse.

It was Cain's fault that his offering was rejected. He was disobedient to God's command to honor Him with the tithe. Cain gave God his leftovers, not his best.

We must always remember that whenever destruction and the Curse come, it is always a result of our disobedience. The enemy is always lying in wait to steal, kill, and destroy. He is waiting for you to give him permission to take you out.

Proverbs 26:2 (NLT) says, "Like a fluttering sparrow or a darting swallow, an undeserved curse will not land on its intended victim."

There is always a reason for destruction and it is always disobedience to the Word.

Look at what Jesus said in John 10:10, He spelled it out for us, He was setting the record straight, *It is the THIEF (Satan) who comes only to steal, kill, and destroy, but Jesus came to give us the overflowing, abundant, more than enough, healthy, whole, wealthy, BLESSED, Zoe life (The God kind of life). A life free from Satan and the curse! Praise God!*

Next time you hear someone blame God for their situation, be bold and correct them. Remind them of how good God is. Remind them that if it wasn't for God's goodness they wouldn't even have breath to fill their lungs.

Teach them the truth found in John 10:10. Set the record straight --- the Devil is the thief and God is the Blesser! Tell them that blaming God for their mess is offensive, because that is not the God that you serve!

Remind them what Psalm 103:1-5 says, "[1]Bless the LORD, O my soul; and all that is within me, bless His holy name! [2] Bless the LORD, O my soul, and *forget not all His benefits:* [3] *Who forgives all your iniquities, Who heals all your diseases,* [4] *Who redeems your life from destruction, Who crowns you with lovingkindness and tender mercies,* [5] *Who satisfies your mouth with good things, so that your youth is renewed like the eagle's.*" (Emphasis Added). Remind them that walking with Our God has many benefits and the Boldly praise Him for His many covenant benefits! GOD IS GOOD — ALL THE TIME — AND ALL THE TIME — GOD IS GOOD!!! AMEN!

Daily Declaration

Thank You Father for Your Blessing on my life! I am so grateful for all that You have done, are doing, and will do in my life! Help me to walk in Your love and to share Your goodness with those I meet every day. I want to be a light in this dark world. I want to help change the false perception and the lies that the enemy has worked so hard for centuries to create about You and Your character. In fact, I want the entire world to know the TRUTH about how Good You are! Lord, You are the love of my life. You are the One who makes life worth living. You are my Joy, my Peace, My Wholeness, my Everything!!! Bless You Lord! I just want to Praise You and tell You just how wonderful You are to me. I love You Lord, and I pray these things in the mighty name of Jesus, Amen.

Day 13
Call It To You

"As it is written, "I have made you a father of many nations" in the presence of Him whom he believed — God, who gives life to the dead and calls those things which do not exist as though they did."

Romans 4:17

I f you wanted to get in touch with a friend who lived hours away, how would you do it? You would most likely pick up the phone and call them. If you wanted a pizza, but didn't want to go to the pizzeria, you would call for delivery. And if you let your dog out of the house into the backyard, but latter wanted him to come back inside, you would open the door and call for him to come to you, right?

Well, whether you know it or not — FAITH works the exact same way. As People of faith we call for things that we desire — things that we don't presently perceive or have in our physical possession — in order to make them manifest in this natural physical realm. Now, I know this might sound a little bit like Star Trek or the Twilight Zone, but let me explain.

This isn't a new idea, in fact, it is a God idea. Notice what Paul says in Romans 4:17-18 (ERV). "17 As the Scriptures say, "I have made you a father of many nations." This is true before God, the one Abraham believed — the God who gives life to the dead *and speaks of things that don't yet exist as if they are real.* 18 There was no hope that Abraham would have children, but Abraham believed God and continued to hope. And that is why he became the father of many nations. As God told him, "You will have many descendants." (Emphasis Added).

In Ephesians 5:1 we are instructed to be imitators of God as His dear children. So if that is how God used His faith to bring about those things He desired, then we should do the same. We have been instructed by God to base our faith in what He has promised us in His Word.

God always calls the things He desires by faith. His creative force is always expressed by the words He speaks. He made covenant with Abram (exalted father) and then called him Abraham (father of nations). God changed Abram's destiny by calling him a father before he ever was.

In other words, He spoke the desired end and it came into being. The reason it took so long for Abraham to become a father was because Abraham had to get God's promise on the inside of him. He had to move from head knowledge to heart knowledge. In other words, God's Word had to become more than just a bunch of words—it had to become an promise that had to become a reality—because God is not a man that He should lie or the son of man that He should repent (See Numbers 23:19).

God's promise had to become bigger and more true than the facts that Abram and Sarah could not biologically conceive children due to their age and physiological limitations.

Jesus did the same thing when He raised Lazarus from the dead in John 11:40-44, "[40] Did I not say to you that if you would believe you would see the glory of God?" [41] Then they took away the stone from the place where the dead man was lying. And Jesus lifted up His eyes and said, "Father, I thank You that You have heard Me. [42] And I know that You always hear Me, but because of the people who are standing by I said this, that they may believe that You sent Me." [43] Now when He had said these things, He cried with a loud voice, "Lazarus, come forth!" [44] And he who had died came out..."

What was the necessary ingredient in order for Mary and Martha to see the glory of God? They had to have FAITH!

Our Heavenly Father did the exact same thing in the beginning when He spoke the world into existence (See Genesis 1).

In 2 Corinthians 4:13 & 18, Paul illustrates this same truth when he writes, "[13] And since we have the same spirit of faith, according to what is written, "I believed and therefore I spoke," we also believe and therefore speak...[18] while we do not look at the things which are seen, but at the things which are not seen. For the things which are seen are temporary, but the things which are not seen are eternal."

The problem most Christians face is that they are paying way too much attention to the things that are seen. They are calling things that are as though they are. These people call their sickness as it is. In fact they have claimed it..."Yes, MY diabetes is acting up." **I want you to know...It's not your diabetes, it's the devils! You don't want it, so don't claim it as yours!**

These same people call poverty to themselves by saying things like, "Man, I'm broke! I'll never get this car paid off...every time I get ahead something breaks and then I'm back to square one." Is that what you want? Then don't be calling it to yourself!

Some denominations criticize this kind of thinking, but they are ignoring the truth of the Bible. How did they receive their salvation? They called it to them! They obeyed Romans 10:6-10 and believed in their heart and confessed with their mouth that Jesus is Lord of their lives.

If there is something you are believing for; find out what the Bible has to say about it. Be diligent and find multiple Scriptures to base your faith and confidence in. Then open your mouth and call it to you!

In Mark 11:22-24 Jesus told His followers to do exactly what I am telling you — when He said, "[22] Have faith in God [or the God kind of faith]. [23] For assuredly, I say to you, whoever says to this mountain, 'Be removed and be cast into the sea,' and does not doubt in his heart, but believes that those things he says will be done, he will have whatever he says. [24] Therefore I say to you, whatever things you ask when you pray, believe that you receive *them,* and you will have *them"*

Them what? Them things you are speaking [it may not be good English, but it true nonetheless], they spoke, called, decreed by faith, believing that they'd received what they had prayed for, the moment that they spoke — and YOU SHOULD TOO! You've been created in God's image and given His authority to rule and reign in this earth. Don't you think it's about time to start doing what He said? I do!

Daily Declaration

In the name of Jesus, I call those things that I am believing for to me (take the time and call them by name). I declare that I have them now! I am not moved by what I see, but I am only moved by what I believe—and I believe the Word of God. I am a child of the Most High God. And As a joint-heir with Christ Jesus, I take my place of authority in Him and declare that I shall lack no good thing, in Jesus' name! Job 22:28 (AMP) says, "You shall also decide and decree a thing, and it shall be established for you; and the light [of God's favor] shall shine upon your ways." I walk in the favor and power of Almighty God and I will not be denied anything that Jesus has already made available to me by faith. I am the righteousness of God in Christ. I am Blessed, and Call God's Blessing to me by faith. Ephesians 3:1 says, "God has blessed us with every spiritual blessing in the heavenly places in Christ." Deuteronomy 28:8 says, God has commanded His Blessing on me." I cannot fail. I cannot lose because Jesus is my Lord, my Help, and my covenant Source. Thank You Father, for bringing this prayer to pass—in Jesus' name, Amen.

Day 14
The Chorus Remains The Same

"For the LORD is good and his love endures forever; his faithfulness continues through all generations."

Psalm 100:5 (NIV)

I n 1950 Harry S. Truman coined the phrase, "Not all readers are leaders, but all leaders are readers." I believe that this statement is true. Reading opens up our eyes to truths that can inspire ideas within us to dream bigger dreams and to believe God to help us accomplish extraordinary exploits. That said; I want to share something that I recently read in Jentezen Franklin's new book *The Spirit of Python*.

In his book pastor Franklin wrote, "Adversity 'adds a verse' to your song, but the chorus remains the same." As I pondered my life and what Jentezen had written, I was reminded of the Casting Crowns song, *Lifesong*. In it, Mark Hall, the lead singer, prays that his life would be a song of praise in God's ear.

The words of that song create powerful imagery in my mind. His prayer is not only requesting that our God receive us into Heaven when we leave this earth, but it is also a declaration that we will worship God during the good and the bad times, trusting that He will see us through every storm. It's an anthem committing to faithfully trust in His love, no matter what our circumstances look like in the natural, because He is our Good and faithful Savior."

Job said it this way, "¹⁵ Though He slay me, yet will I trust Him. Even so, I will defend my own ways before Him. ¹⁶ He also shall be my salvation, for a hypocrite could not come before Him. ¹⁷ Listen carefully to my speech, and to my declaration with your ears. ¹⁸ See now, I have prepared my case, I know that I shall be vindicated." (See Job 13:15-18).

In this passage, Job is giving his rebuttal to his critics. They have all suggested that the chaos he is enduring is the result of his sins, a sure sign that God is mad at him, and that he should just curse God and die. But just as King David declared of God throughout the Psalms, Job also understood the truth of God's character and Satan's. The truth was — Job's critics were wrong — God wasn't mad at Job and He's not mad at you either!

In the very first verse of Job Chapter 1 we read, "There was a man in the land of Uz, whose name was Job; and *that man was blameless and upright, and one who feared God [reverenced Him] and shunned evil.*" (Emphasis Added).

Job was a RIGHTEOUS man! When are we going to begin to understand that God is a GOOD God and the Devil is a BAD Devil? Bad things happen to good people because as 1 Peter 5:8-9 (NLT) explains — there is an evil predator loose, looking for his next meal. "⁸ Stay alert! Watch out for your great enemy, the devil. He prowls around like a roaring lion, looking for someone to devour. ⁹ Stand firm against him, and be strong in your faith. Remember that your Christian brothers and sisters all over the world are going through the same kind of suffering you are."

We must also remember what John 10:10 tells us, "The thief does not come except to steal, and to kill, and to destroy…" Satan's mission is to try to take us out and then convince us that it was God who hurt us. Satan wants us to believe the lie that God hurt us in order to teach us a lesson, but don't fall for his garbage—the Devil's a LIAR!

Just like Pastor Franklin said in his book, every time adversity comes our way, every time trials occur in our lives, and people are encouraging us to blame God and throw in our towel, instead of listening to those naysayers—just add another verse to your life song.

King David was famous for adding verses to his life song. In Psalm 138:1-5 (NIV) David sang, "[1] I will praise you, LORD, with all my heart; before the "gods" I will sing your praise. [2] I will bow down toward your holy temple and will praise your name for your unfailing love and your faithfulness, for you have so exalted your solemn decree that it surpasses your fame. [3] When I called, you answered me; you greatly emboldened me. [4] May all the kings of the earth praise you, LORD, when they hear what you have decreed. [5] May they sing of the ways of the LORD, for the glory of the LORD is great."

Notice all of the verses that David added to his life song in Psalm 136 and then recognize his chorus which always remained the same. "[1] Oh, give thanks to the LORD, for He is good! For His mercy endures forever. [2] Oh, give thanks to the God of gods! For His mercy endures forever. [3] Oh, give thanks to the Lord of lords! For His mercy endures forever: [4] To Him who alone does great wonders, for His mercy endures forever; [5] To Him who by wisdom made the heavens, for His mercy endures forever; [6] To Him who laid out the earth above the waters, for His mercy endures forever; [7] To Him who made great lights, for His mercy endures forever— [8] The sun to rule by day, for His mercy endures forever; [9] The moon and stars to rule by night, for His mercy endures forever. [10] To Him who struck Egypt in their firstborn, for His mercy endures forever; [11] And brought out Israel from among them, for His mercy endures forever; [12] With a strong hand, and with an outstretched arm, for His mercy endures forever; [13] To Him who divided the Red Sea in two, for His mercy endures forever; [14] And made Israel pass through the midst of it, for His mercy endures forever; [15] But overthrew Pharaoh and his army in the Red Sea, for His mercy endures forever; [16] To Him who led His people through the wilderness, for His mercy endures forever; [17] To Him who struck down great kings, for His mercy endures forever; [18] And slew famous kings, for His mercy endures forever — [19] Sihon king of the Amorites, for His mercy endures forever; [20] And Og king of Bashan, for His mercy endures forever — [21] And gave their land as a heritage, for His mercy endures forever; [22] A heritage to Israel His servant, for His mercy endures forever. [23] Who remembered us in our lowly state, for His mercy endures forever; [24] And rescued us from our enemies, for His mercy endures forever; [25] Who gives food to all flesh, for His mercy endures forever. [26] Oh, give thanks to the God of heaven! For His mercy endures forever." (Psalm 136:1-26).

In 2 Samuel 22:1-7 we read, "Then David spoke to the LORD the words of this song, on the day when the LORD had delivered him from the hand of all his enemies, and from the hand of Saul. [2] And he said: "The LORD is My rock and My fortress and My deliverer; [3] The God of My strength, in whom I will trust; My shield and the horn of My salvation, My stronghold and My refuge; My Savior, You save me from violence. [4] I will call upon the LORD, who is worthy to be praised; so shall I be saved from my enemies. [5] "When the waves of death surrounded me, the floods of ungodliness made me afraid. [6] The sorrows of Sheol surrounded me; the snares of death confronted me. [7] In my distress I called upon the LORD, and cried out to my God; He heard my voice from His temple, and my cry entered His ears."

The question that you must ask yourself right now is— "Is God **Your** rock, **Your** fortress, **Your** deliverer? Is He the God of **Your** strength? Is He **Your** shield, the Horn of **Your** salvation, **Your** stronghold, **Your** refuge, and **Your** Savior?" If you're trying to do it all on your own, in your own strength, then He isn't—You're trying to be your own God.

If we continue reading through 2 Samuel 22:17-20 we see that David continues his song of praise by singing, "[17] He sent from above, He took me, He drew me out of many waters. [18] He delivered me from my strong enemy, from those who hated me; for they were too strong for me. [19] They confronted me in the day of my calamity, *but the LORD was my support.* [20] *He also brought me out into a broad place*; He delivered me because He delighted in me."

I want to declare to you today: *God is your Support, He is your Defender, your Deliverer, and He is bringing you out into a BROAD PLACE. He's bringing you into a place of refreshing, a place of beauty for your ashes, and a place of healing, comfort, and prosperity – spirit, soul, and body. He's bringing you into a place that will restore the years that the locusts have eaten. And into a place that will thrill your spirit and add another verse of praise to your life song.*

The last verse that was added to your life song may have been a little somber, but get ready to clap your hands and to stomp your feet because the tempo is getting ready to rise. Soon enough you'll be singing your new verses, but you'll also be singing the triumphant chorus and shouting your praises of victory, your praises concerning His goodness and His FAVOR which is operating in your life, and your praises about His awesome faithfulness and unfailing love. You may add a new verse to your life song here and there, but the CHORUS ALWAYS REMAINS THE SAME – "For the LORD is good and his love endures forever…"

OUR GOD IS A GOOD GOD! Continue singing His songs of praise! When Adversity strikes, strike back by adding a verse of praise to your Life Song—and Praise your way through the storm!

Daily Declaration

Father, I thank You for Your faithfulness in my life. If I can attest to anything, it is that You have never let me down. You **_ALWAYS_** do exactly what You have promised—and I am grateful for all You do. I desperately want You to know how much I love You Lord. You are my all-in-all. No matter what I experience in life I know beyond a shadow of a doubt that You are for me and that You love me. Jesus warned us in John 16:33 (GWT), "I told you this so that My peace will be with you. In the world you will have trouble. But cheer up! I have overcome the world." Hallelujah! That is wonderful news. If Jesus has overcome the world and lives inside me—then I have overcome the world too! This means that there may be different verses in the life I live, but the chorus will ALWAYS remain the same—I WIN. Because just as David, "[I will], give thanks to the LORD, for He is good! For His mercy endures forever. [2] [I will], give thanks to the God of gods! For His mercy endures forever. [3] [I will], give thanks to the Lord of lords! For His mercy endures forever: [4] To Him who alone does great wonders, for His mercy endures forever." (Psalm 136:1-4). I pray these things in Jesus' mighty name, Amen.

Day 15
You Are A Light In The Midst Of Darkness

"Behold, I send you out as sheep in the midst of wolves.
Therefore be wise as serpents and harmless as doves."

Matthew 10:16

What do you think of when you read the verse above? I believe that most of us see the obvious contrast between good and evil. Most people probably also see the connection between the Garden of Eden and the Fall of Man. Some are probably even reminded of the perilous times that will come during the last days and during the tribulation—where there will be great persecution of Christians because of their faith in Jesus Christ. But how many of us recognize the advantage that light always has over darkness? Darkness cannot remain where the light is—light drives the darkness away.

In John 8:12 Jesus explains who He is and who we are in Him, "Then Jesus spoke to them again, saying, "I am the light of the world. He who follows Me shall not walk in darkness, but have the light of life."

In Matthew 5:13-15, Jesus explains the kind of life Believers are supposed to exhibit in this dark world, "13 You are the salt of the earth; but if the salt loses its flavor, how shall it be seasoned? It is then good for nothing but to be thrown out and trampled underfoot by men. 14 You are the light of the world. A city that is set on a hill cannot be hidden. [15] Nor do they light a lamp and put it under a basket, but on a lampstand, and it gives light to all who are in the house. [16] Let your light so shine before men, that they may see your good works and glorify your Father in heaven."

We are here for a purpose! We're are here to shine the light of God and to attract those who are lost in darkness, encouraging them to receive the light for themselves. There are those however, who don't want the message of Jesus and the hope we have in Him to be spread. This antichrist spirit began way back in the Garden of Eden with the temptation of man by Satan disguised as a serpent.

In Genesis 3:1-6 we read, "[1]Now the serpent was more cunning than any beast of the field which the LORD God had made. And he said to the woman, "Has God indeed said, 'You shall not eat of every tree of the garden'?" [2] And the woman said to the serpent, "We may eat the fruit of the trees of the garden; [3] but of the fruit of the tree which is in the midst of the garden, God has said, 'You shall not eat it, nor shall you touch it, lest you die.'" [4] Then the serpent said to the woman, "You will not surely die. [5] For God knows that in the day you eat of it your eyes will be opened, and you will be like God, knowing good and evil." [6] So when the woman saw that the tree was good for food, that it was pleasant to the eyes, and a tree desirable to make one wise, she took of its fruit and ate. She also gave to her husband with her, and he ate."

The enemy is always crafty in the ways he attacks. He uses subtle tactics to distract and deceive unsuspecting prey. The Hebrew word for serpent used in Genesis 3:1 is *nahasch*, which means serpent, snake, or viper. *Nachash*, also has a more subtle meaning however that sheds more light on the tactics that Satan uses in his assault against humans — these devious devices are similar to those that poisonous vipers like the rattlesnake uses to kill its prey.

The rattlesnake not only uses its rattle as a tool to ward off potential threats, but it also uses its rattle as a means to distract its victims. This cunning maneuver enables the snake to capture the attention of its unsuspecting prey, pretending to be harmless or surprised, yet then it then slithers in from behind, to unleash the fatal blow.

Sin is very much the same as a rattlesnakes rattle. It always tries to sell itself as being pleasurable through its distracting and enticing promises, but these sly lures are never what they portray themselves to be, and they always lead to destruction.

In 1 John 2:15-17, John instructs us to be cautious of the hidden agendas which the enemy often disguises through his crafty schemes. In this passage John writes, "15 Do not love the world or the things in the world. If anyone loves the world, the love of the Father is not in him. 16 For all that is in the world — the lust of the flesh, the lust of the eyes, and the pride of life — is not of the Father but is of the world. 17 And the world is passing away, and the lust of it; but he who does the will of God abides forever."

Instead of falling into the trap of sin, we are to be aware of the devils tactics and to run directly into the light of the Word which always reveals the truth, and to walk in the light as God is in the light.

1 John 1:5-7 says, "5 This is the message which we have heard from Him and declare to you, that God is light and in Him is no darkness at all. 6 If we say that we have fellowship with Him, and walk in darkness, we lie and do not practice

the truth. ⁷But if we walk in the light as He is in the light, we have fellowship with one another, and the blood of Jesus Christ His Son cleanses us from all sin."

Ephesians 5:8-15 clarifies further stating , "⁸For you were once darkness, but now you are light in the Lord. Walk as children of light...¹¹ And have no fellowship with the unfruitful works of darkness, but rather expose them...¹³ But all things that are exposed are made manifest by the light, for whatever makes manifest is light. ¹⁴Therefore He says: "Awake, you who sleep, arise from the dead, and Christ will give you light." ¹⁵See then that you walk circumspectly, not as fools but as wise, ¹⁶ redeeming the time, because the days are evil."

Walking circumspectly simply means to walk cautiously, watchfully, carefully, or vigilantly, always looking suspiciously around ourselves for signs of an impending ambush by the enemy.

1 Peter 5:8-9 explains why we are to be so cautious, "⁸ Be sober, be vigilant; because your adversary the devil walks about like a roaring lion, seeking whom he may devour. ⁹ Resist him, steadfast in the faith, knowing that the same sufferings are experienced by your brotherhood in the world."

The devil hates our guts. His mission is to steal, to kill, and to destroy us when given the opportunity. The problem is however, that he doesn't have the authority to do so unless we give it to him by opening up a door through our sin.

1 Peter 5:9 is not suggesting that suffering is mandatory in this life, instead Peter is warning us to be cautious, because even those people who we put on pedestals for their faithfulness and obedience to God, are sometimes deceived or out smarted by the enemy, through his cunning tactics and

subtle schemes.

Another example of the enemy's underhanded maneuvers is shared by the Apostle Paul in Romans 16:17-20 , "[17] Now I urge you, brethren, note those who cause divisions and offenses, contrary to the doctrine which you learned, and avoid them. [18] For those who are such do not serve our Lord Jesus Christ, but their own belly, and by smooth words and flattering speech deceive the hearts of the simple. [19] For your obedience has become known to all. Therefore I am glad on your behalf; but I want you to be wise in what is good, and simple concerning evil. [20] And the God of peace will crush Satan under your feet shortly."

I would encourage you to be weary, but not to be fearful concerning Satan's techniques to trap you in sin. Don't be like Eve or other unsuspecting brothers and sisters in Christ who are blinded to his sly schemes. Don't be like those who are deceived by the melodic sound of the enemies rattle only to be caught off guard and fall victim to his trap. Satan is crafty but he has three main modes of deception which he uses to capture and kill his prey: the lust of the flesh, the lust of the eyes, and the pride of life.

Instead of falling victim to his conniving schemes remain vigilant and, "Be wise as serpents and harmless as doves...and walk in the light as He is in the light"

Daily Declaration

I declare that I am a light in this dark world because Jesus shines bright inside of me. The Bible says that I am in this world, but not of it. I have been translated out of darkness and sin into His glorious light. I am the redeemed of the Lord and I say so. Jesus paid the price to free me from my sin and to cleanse me of all unrighteousness. Satan, I bind you in the name of Jesus and render you harmless and ineffective against me in Jesus' mighty name. I plead the Blood of Jesus over myself, my family, and over everything that concerns me and in doing so; I declare them off limits to any demonic attack or devious plot. Holy Spirit, I ask You to lead and guide me into all truth. Romans 8:1 tells me that I am no longer bound by guilt, condemnation, or shame therefore, I refuse everything that doesn't belong to me in Jesus' name. And in Romans 8:26-30 I am told, "[26] Likewise the Spirit also helps in our weaknesses. For we do not know what we should pray for as we ought, but the Spirit Himself makes intercession for us with groanings which cannot be uttered. [27] Now He who searches the hearts knows what the mind of the Spirit is, because He makes intercession for the saints according to the will of God. [28] And we know that all things work together for good to those who love God, to those who are the called according to His purpose. [29] For whom He foreknew, He also predestined to be conformed to the image of His Son, that He might be the firstborn among many brethren. [30] Moreover whom He predestined, these He also called; whom He called, these He also justified; and whom He justified, these He also glorified. I pray these things in Jesus' name, Amen.

Day 16
No Fear Here!

"For God has not given us a spirit of fear, but of power and of love and of a sound mind."

2 Timothy 1:7

Years ago, my spiritual father in the faith, Kenneth Copeland, had a slogan regarding fear: "No Fear Here!" In fact, he taught on fear for a number of years, explaining that fear is a spiritual force that connects a person to Satan and the Curse, just like faith is a spiritual force that connects a person to God and the Blessing.

Hebrews 11:6 explains, "But without faith it is impossible to please Him [God], for he who comes to God must believe that He is, and that He is a rewarder of those who diligently seek Him.

Fear works the same way faith does. Just as faith comes by hearing the Word of God (Romans 10:17), fear comes by hearing the lies of Satan. In fact, fear is the reciprocal of faith or faith in reverse. You could correctly say, "Without fear it is impossible to please Satan, for whoever comes to Satan must doubt God and His Word, because Satan is the curser, the thief, and the destroyer of dreams and lives."

The word wicked literally means to be twisted. Think about wicker furniture, it is made from twisted wood. What about a candle wick? It is made from twisted string. Satan is not a creator of anything, but a fraud who twists the truth of God and deceives people into believing his lies.

Notice what he did with Eve in the garden? Now the serpent was more cunning than any beast of the field which the LORD God had made. *And he said to the woman, "Has God indeed said, 'You shall not eat of every tree of the garden'?"* [2] And the woman said to the serpent, "We may eat the fruit of the trees of the garden; [3] but of the fruit of the tree which *is* in the midst of the garden, God has said, 'You shall not eat it, nor shall you touch it, lest you die.'" [4] *Then the serpent said to the woman, "You will not surely die. [5] For God knows that in the day you eat of it your eyes will be opened, and you will be like God, knowing good and evil."* (Emphasis Added).

The devil (that serpent) asked Eve questions and then twisted the truth trying to create doubt and fear in her mind about God's goodness...as a result, fear crept in and Eve was deceived.

I want you to know that Satan plays those same lying games with us, twisting the truth, and trying to convince us that God doesn't love us or that God won't or can't help us out of our negative circumstances. But GUESS AGAIN! HE'S A LIAR! He's up to his old trickery trying to instil fear in you so that he can destroy you. But in order for his plan to work, he needs your cooperation—he needs your permission to accomplish his task!

Why is fear so bad for the believer? As I explained earlier—fear connects us to the Curse, but faith connects us to LOVE.

In 1 John 4:8; 16, we learn that God is LOVE. And in 1 Corinthians 13:4-8 (NIV), we are shown the characteristics of Love, "[4] Love is patient, love is kind. It does not envy, it does not boast, it is not proud. [5] It does not dishonor others, it is not self-seeking, it is not easily angered, it keeps no record of wrongs. [6] Love does not delight in evil but rejoices with the truth. [7] It always protects, always trusts, always hopes, always perseveres. [8] Love never fails."

In first John 4:17-18 we learn more about the differences between love and fear, [17] Love has been perfected among us [Believers] in this: that we may have boldness in the day of judgment; because as He is, so are we in this world [we've been created in His image to operate as He does]. [18] There is no fear in love; but perfect love casts out fear, because fear involves torment. But he who fears has not been made perfect in love [in God, who is Love].

Because fear is twisted faith or faith in reverse, when we allow fear to operate in our lives, we are literally telling God that we don't believe a word He's promised us in the Bible. Allowing fear to remain in operation illustrates to God that we believe that the devil is bigger and more powerful than He is. It shows Him that we believe that He is not capable of helping us out of our messes.

If you think about it, Allowing fear access into our lives is like spitting in God's face. What an insult! As a result of allowing fear access, fear then turns into torment, worry, and anxiety. The end result of meditating on the negative (on the lies of the devil) then lead to fear growing bigger and finally, as Job declared in Job 3:25, "For the thing I greatly feared has come upon me, and what I dreaded has happened to me."

How does that happen? It happens because fear draws it to you through the thoughts and words you speak, through your actions, and by unknowingly creating what you believe in your heart.

Proverbs 23:7 says, "For as he thinks in his heart, so is he." Through your negative meditations and spoken words you give FEAR permission to operate in your life. And since fear connects us directly to Satan and his Curse, those actions allow the lying images of defeat, lack, sickness, unworthiness, etc., to manifest in your life. Fear always causes us to magnify the problems in our lives instead of magnifying the solutions promised in God's Word!

So what should we do? We should put on the amour of the God so that we can guard against every demonic attack. Ephesians 6:10-13 says, "[10] Finally, my brethren, be strong in the Lord and in the power of His might. [11] *Put on the whole armor of God, that you may be able to stand against the wiles of the devil.* [12] For we do not wrestle against flesh and blood, but against principalities, against powers, against the rulers of the darkness of this age, against spiritual hosts of wickedness in the heavenly places. [13] *Therefore take up the whole armor of God, that you may be able to withstand in the evil day, and having done all, to stand." (Emphasis Added).*

Next we need to cast down vain imaginations, 2 Corinthians 10:3-5 (KJV) tells us, "[3]For though we walk in the flesh, we do not war after the flesh: [4](For the weapons of our warfare are not carnal, but mighty through God to the pulling down of strong holds;) [5]Casting down imaginations, and every high thing that exalteth itself against the knowledge of God, and bringing into captivity every thought to the obedience of Christ."

Anytime the enemy attacks with thoughts of loss, lack, fear, defeat—CAST THEM DOWN! Tell the devil that those aren't your thoughts and then tell him to flee in the name of Jesus!

God has not given you the spirit of fear! And if He didn't give it to you then you don't have to receive it! Hallelujah! God has given you the Spirit of power through Jesus, the Blood, His name. He's given you the Spirit of Love — His Spirit, and He's given you a mind free from Fear and the Curse.

Don't settle for less than what God has given you! When fear comes creeping in tell Satan to scram! Then begin to feed on and to build-up your faith in the Word.

Mark Hankins says, "When faith cometh, fear goeth!" Kick fear completely out of your life with the Word of God and walk in the power, authority, love, and soundness that your Heavenly Father created you to walk in. YOU HAVE THE VICTORY IN JESUS! AMEN!

Daily Declaration

Father, I declare that there is NO FEAR HERE, in Jesus' name! I bind fear from operating in my life. Lord, You haven't given me the spirit of fear, so therefore, I refuse to receive anything that is not from You. I put on the whole armor of God so that I can stand in the midst of every attack. I am Blessed with every spiritual Blessing in Christ Jesus! I declare that I will speak only words of faith and words of love. I have the mind of Christ, and therefore, any thought that does not line-up with the Word of God, I cast it down and refuse it access in Jesus name. My body, mind, and spirit are the temple of God. I will not allow any foreign and false idols to take up residence in this temple.

Father, I thank You for setting a guard about me—a hedge of protection which denies the enemy access. I clearly understand from Job's life that Satan's goal is to tear down that hedge and gain access into my life so that he can then steal, kill, and destroy me. But I also know the truth: He can't tear it down unless I allow it. In Job 1:9-10 (MSG) Satan goes to God trying to convince Him to tear down the hedge of protection surrounding Job saying, "So do you think Job does all that out of the sheer goodness of his heart? Why, *no one ever had it so good!* You pamper him like a pet, make sure nothing bad ever happens to him or his family or his possessions, *[You] bless everything he does—he can't lose!"* This must mean that Satan had tried to take that wall down many times before but couldn't. But what we discover next is very interesting, in Job 1:12 God tells Satan, "Behold, all that he has is in your power; only do not lay a hand on his person." Why? Because Job was operating in fear.   We know this because of what we read in Job 1:5, "⁵ So it was, when the days of feasting had run their course, that Job would send and sanctify them, and *he would rise early in the morning and offer burnt offerings* according to the number of them all. For Job said, "It may be that my sons have sinned and cursed God in their hearts." ***Thus Job did regularly.***" (Emphasis Added).

Do you see it? Job would rise early and offer burnt OFFERINGS—which Job did REGULARLY. In other words, there was no faith in his actions. He didn't make his offering and stand on the promises of God—he made multiple offerings hoping that if the first 10 or 12 didn't work that maybe another one would.

That's fear my friends and it will kill you. You've got to know that when you do what God has commanded—it will work! You have to have the confidence that God's promises won't return void in your life.

1 John 5:14-15 (AMP) says, "¹⁴ And this is the confidence (the assurance, the privilege of boldness) which we have in Him: [we are sure] that if we ask anything (make any request) according to His will (in agreement with His own plan), He listens to and hears us. ¹⁵ And if (since) we [positively] know that He listens to us in whatever we ask, we also know [with settled and absolute knowledge] that we have [granted us as our present possessions] the requests made of Him."

Father, I trust in Your Word! I believe it will work for my just as You promised. And I know that unless I give the devil access, he can't take me out. I bless You Lord and pray these things in Jesus' mighty name, Amen.

Day 17
Peace — The Guardian Of Your Heart & Mind

"⁶ Be anxious for nothing, but in everything by prayer and supplication, with thanksgiving, let your requests be made known to God; ⁷ and the peace of God, which surpasses all understanding, will guard your hearts and minds through Christ Jesus."

Philippians 4:6-7

W here does real peace come from? It comes from knowing God, knowing that our Source and Supply has heard our prayers and is actively bringing them to pass just like He promised He would. It comes from knowing His love and understanding that He will NEVER leave us or forsake us under any circumstance.

The amazing thing is that when we know that our prayers have been heard — we are filled with an immoveable confidence. Confidence is simply a strong knowing on the inside which confirms that no matter how bad things may look right now — they can't stay that way. It's an unshakeable trust that says, "If God is for me, then who can stand against me?"

Another way to explain this confidence and peace is to say that it's a strong belief deep on the inside which causes us to agree with 2 Corinthians 2:14 and shout, "But thanks be to God, who always leads us in victory through Christ."

The foundation for this wonderful peace is based on the understanding that the Father loves me just as much as He loves Jesus, and knowing that I share equally in all God has. In fact, in John 17:23, Jesus prayed that we might understand the Fathers love for us. And in Romans 8:16-17, Paul explains to us that we are God's children and that we share equally in all that Jesus owns because He is the mediator of the covenant promises.

As heirs of the covenant promises, Colossians 3:15-17 encourages us to, "[15] Let the peace that Christ gives control your thinking. It is for peace that you were chosen to be together in one body. And always be thankful. [16] Let the teaching of Christ live inside you richly. Use all wisdom to teach and counsel each other. Sing psalms, hymns, and spiritual songs with thankfulness in your hearts to God. [17] Everything you say and everything you do should be done for Jesus your Lord. And in all you do, give thanks to God the Father through Jesus."

When we focus on the things of God instead of on the things of the Curse, we are then destined to live in the BLESSING—God's original plan for our lives.

In Isaiah 26:3 we read, "You [oh God] will keep him in perfect peace, whose mind is stayed on You, because he trusts in You."

Is there anyone better to trust in than the Creator of the universe? Of course not! He can change any situation we face if we just give Him a little faith to work with. But that is the key—we play a part in having our prayers answered. We must operate in faith (confident trust) believing God and His Word, if we want our prayers to come to pass.

Moreover, we are not only responsible for adding our faith to God's Word, but Philippians4:6-7 tells us that we are to stamp out all fear, worry, and doubt. When we obey and cast down all devious imaginations that don't line-up with the Bible, then God's unsurpassing peace mounts a guard over our hearts and over our minds.

With Peace as the guard over our spirit and mind, no tactic of the enemy will ever be successful at getting to us and overthrowing our dreams, desires, or destiny.

That's why it is so important to let peace rule in our hearts as Colossians 3:15-17 (AMP) instructs. "[15] And let the peace (soul harmony which comes) from Christ rule (act as umpire continually) in your hearts [deciding and settling with finality all questions that arise in your minds, in that peaceful state] to which as [members of Christ's] one body you were also called [to live]. And be thankful (appreciative), [giving praise to God always].[16] Let the word [spoken by] Christ (the Messiah) have its home [in your hearts and minds] and dwell in you in [all its] richness, as you teach and admonish and train one another in all insight and intelligence and wisdom [in spiritual things, and as you sing] psalms and hymns and spiritual songs, making melody to God with [His] grace in your hearts. [17] And whatever you do [no matter what it is] in word or deed, do everything in the name of the Lord Jesus and in [dependence upon] His Person, giving praise to God the Father through Him."

When we quit trying to fight our own battles then we get out of God's way and He fights them for us. Our job isn't to make things happen in our own strength, but our job is to believe those things God has already promised us in the Bible. We are called to receive those precious promises by faith and then to rest in our confidence and in the perfect peace of God living fear free. We are Children of the Most High God and as such, we are joint heirs with Christ, victorious in Jesus, and we are called to enjoy the fruit — the PEACE — of the BLESSED LIFE!

Daily Declaration

Father, I declare that I live a worry-free life of peace surrounded by Your all surpassing goodness and favor. I put on peace as a guard over my heart and my mind. The Bible promises me that no weapon formed against me shall prosper. (See Isaiah 54:17). I believe your promises and I stand in confident trust and expectation, believing to receive the fulfillment of Your promises in my life. I have the mind of Christ and I allow peace to rule in my life as an umpire. I am not anxious about anything, but in all things through prayer and thanksgiving I make all of my requests known to You Lord, and as a result Your peace comes over me and washes away all of the cares of this life. Thank You Lord, for taking such good care of me and for loving me as much as You love Jesus. I receive all that You have for me, and I bless Your holy name. I pray these things in Jesus' name, Amen.

Day 18
I Believe Lord...Only Speak A Word

"⁷ And Jesus said to him, "I will come and heal him." ⁸ The centurion answered and said, "Lord, I am not worthy that You should come under my roof. But only speak a word, and my servant will be healed. ⁹ For I also am a man under authority, having soldiers under me. And I say to this one, 'Go,' and he goes; and to another, 'Come,' and he comes; and to my servant, 'Do this,' and he does it." ¹⁰ When Jesus heard it, He marveled, and said to those who followed, "Assuredly, I say to you, I have not found such great faith, not even in Israel! ¹¹ And I say to you that many will come from east and west, and sit down with Abraham, Isaac, and Jacob in the kingdom of heaven. ¹² But the sons of the kingdom will be cast out into outer darkness. There will be weeping and gnashing of teeth." ¹³ Then Jesus said to the centurion, "Go your way; and as you have believed, so let it be done for you." And his servant was healed that same hour."

Matthew 8:7-13

How certain are YOU that the Word works every time it is spoken in faith? There is no doubt in my mind that every word of the Bible is absolutely true. I know beyond a shadow of a doubt, that the Word of God is the strongest truth anywhere in the universe. I am sold on the fact that Jesus is Lord over ALL and that if I will believe and act on what He has said, I will have what He has promised to me.

Do you have that same kind of confidence in God's Word or are you drifting back and forth between what you see and feel through your five senses, and the truth of God's precious promises?

I haven't always been this confident in God's Word; in fact at times, my faith (or lack of faith) has been pathetic. There have been times when I have done all I "felt" I could to believe, and caved in to my screaming senses that where telling me, *You're a fool for believing in something you can't see!*

Mark 9:22-24 illustrates this for us. It's a story of a father whose son is possessed by demons and has been that way since childhood. This father has gone to everyone he could find for help, but no one could do anything to free his son from the demonic oppression—that is until he comes to Jesus.

In the passage we are told that Jesus listens patiently as the father describes how the demons try to kill his son saying, "22 And often he has thrown him both into the fire and into the water to destroy him. But if You can do anything, have compassion on us and help us." 23 Jesus said to him, "If you can believe, all things are possible to him who believes." 24 Immediately the father of the child cried out and said with tears, "Lord, I believe; help my unbelief!"

Can you hear the anxiety and tinge of doubt in the father's voice? "I'm believing as much as I possibly can Lord, I've heard the stories about the great miracles you have done for others, but…"

This father is desperately trying to remain strong and faithful, but his past experiences are telling him that this time will be no different from all of the others…just another failed attempt only to return home facing the same bondage.

Yet in his quiet desperation, the father stirs up the courage to ask, "If you can do anything..." I can sense the shame and guilt he must feel for not having more faith to believe for his miracle. He's been down this road before. Are the stories he's heard true or are they just that — stories?

Jesus, the compassionate shepherd that He is turns the responsibility back to the father, "If you can believe, all things are possible to him who believes."

Immediately, the father sees the opportunity he has been waiting for. He understands that Jesus has just made him a covenant promise — a vow which can never be broken, but requires the responsibility of both parties involved. Accepting the terms of the agreement, this loving father cries out with tears, "Lord, I believe; help my unbelief!" A moment later, the boy is completely restored!

Now let's go to Matthew Chapter 8 and look at a similar story about a centurion and his dying servant. Though both of these stories are about Jesus healing two people who have been plagued with demonic attacks, there is a huge difference between the two men asking Jesus for a miracle.

Unlike the father of the sick boy, the centurion has no doubt in his heart that Jesus is who He says He is. The centurion is confident that Jesus can heal his servant if He just speaks a word.

In fact, the centurion tells Jesus, "I don't need any other proof that what You say will occur, other than hearing You say the words...I know that if You just say the Word, it will be done!"

James 1:17 (MSG) says, "Every desirable and beneficial gift comes out of heaven. The gifts are rivers of light cascading down from the Father of Light. There is nothing deceitful in God, nothing two-faced, nothing fickle." In other words, if God said it…it's a done deal!

Jesus recognized the centurion's faith as "GREAT FAITH," in fact, Jesus marveled at his faith (He was amazed with the confidence the centurion placed in His Word). Why? Because most people wanted some sort of sign signifying that He would honor His Word to them — they wanted proof. They wanted to watch Him perform the miracle and then they wanted to critique how He did it, but not the centurion. This great man of faith believed and said, "Just speak a Word Jesus…I believe."

Wouldn't it be great if the things you've been believing God for, would come that quickly? Well they can! Jesus is saying the same thing to you and me that He said to the centurion — "I will come…" But at the same time He's asking us if we have GREAT FAITH or are we like one of those He rebuked for having no faith at all?

Jesus wants to answer your prayer request today, but He has put the responsibility of faith square on your shoulders. Give Him your faith and then listen for Him to say, "Go your way; and as you have believed, so let it be done for you." Isn't God so good?

Daily Declaration

I declare that I am a believer not a doubter and that I have world-overcoming faith. I have the faith to move mountains because I belong to Jesus and have put my complete trust in Him. I guard my spirit against doubt and unbelief and I cast down every thought that tries to exalt itself against the knowledge of Christ and bringing every thought into captivity to the obedience of Christ. (See 2 Corinthians 10:5). The Bible is the final authority for my life. If the Bible says it, I believe it, and that settles it. I know that God's Word will not return void to me because He is not a man that He should lie (See Numbers 23:19). God's Word always comes to pass—it ALWAYS accomplishes what it has been sent out to do. Thank You for Your Word Father. Sanctify me by Your Word Lord; Your Word is THE ONLY TRUTH! (See John 17:17). I pray these things in Jesus' name, Amen.

Day 19
So All Will Know It Was God

"²¹ Now the king of Sodom said to Abram, "Give me the persons [*nephesh* (Hebrew) the souls of the people], and take the goods for yourself." ²² But Abram said to the king of Sodom, "I have raised my hand to the LORD, God Most High, the Possessor of heaven and earth, ²³ that I will take nothing, from a thread to a sandal strap, and that I will not take anything that is yours, lest you should say, 'I have made Abram rich' — ²⁴ except only what the young men have eaten, and the portion of the men who went with me...""

Genesis 14:21-24

Right before we read this passage in Genesis, we find Abram offering the tithe to Melchizedek [translated King of Righteousness] the High Priest and King of Salem. The word Salem comes from the root word Shalom, which is translated as "peace" in English. Jerusalem [or Yireh Salem] could easily be translated the city of provision and peace.

You are probably familiar with one of God's names — Jehovah Jireh, which is often translated as the Lord is my provider. In Hebrew there is no letter "J" instead, the Hebrew spelling of Jehovah Jireh is Yahweh Yireh, which literally means: the God who sees beforehand and therefore provides.

The reason I have bothered to make this point is to prove what Scripture says in Isaiah 46:9-10, "…For I am God, and there is no other; I am God, and there is none like Me, ¹⁰ Declaring the end from the beginning, and from ancient times things that are not yet done…"

Simply put, God knows the end from the beginning; He knows everything we need before we even know that we will need it and He knows what will happen long before it occurs — that's just part of what being God is all about.

That said; we need to trust that He has our best interest in mind and that He will take care of all we need, even when things are chaotic and don't seem to be going as we have planned.

I am positive I'm not the only one who's ever wondered why things have sometimes not gone the way I wanted them to. Every one of us has experienced delays in receiving answers to our prayers. But that's not the time to give up on our faith. If we give up every time things get tough then we will forfeit the Blessing.

I whole-heartedly believe in the Biblical Law of Seedtime and Harvest which is found in (Genesis 8:22). This Spiritual Law states that in order to receive anything in life whether natural or spiritual, there must first be a seed that is sown.

My wife Patty and I have spent years sowing our time, our hearts, our love and our finances into a number of ministries, in the hopes of seeing lives transformed by the Gospel of Jesus.

We have also spent years training those we have had the privilege of pastoring, to believe the Word of God and to be led by the Holy Spirit. We have poured everything we have into ministry and experienced some truly amazing miracles, yet it would be easy to become frustrated in a few areas. It would be easy to become jealous of other ministries we have helped — who have grown faster and have been able to do more than we have.

In fact we are very aware that if we are not careful, the enemy could easily creep in and try to twist our thinking. But we are familiar with his tactics and refuse to allow strife or jealousy to take root in our lives.

There was a time not so long ago that we were believing God for $200,000 for a ministry project we were working towards. We had been praying, sowing into ministries that we felt led by God to sow into, and believing Him to supply our need.

After sowing our seed for our harvest, our church linked arms with another church in our community and went door to door with them praying for people and inviting them to attend an event that ministry was putting on in the community.

Patty and I had recently left Tulsa, Oklahoma where we both worked for a large media ministry that had two weekly television programs that they put together each week. We had served the senior pastor and those who attended the church for a number of years, pouring our time, our hearts, our finances, and our faith to see lives transformed.

In fact, during those years, I never received a salary for the work that I put in on a daily basis. But I sowed my time as a seed believing that God would bring someone to help us once we planted our own church.

My position at the ministry consisted of doing all of the counseling and leading the pastoral care ministry. I had been promised a salary, but it just never came to fruition. Instead, I got a job throwing newspapers 7 days a week and working in a 5 star steak house to pay our bills. This was on top of taking 21 to 23 units of graduate college studies and my work at the church.

The only reason I mention that is to illustrate that we do what we need to do and trust God for the things we need and desire.

Getting back to my story, our church was believing for $200,000 for a ministry project. We had many faithful people who gave selflessly, and most of the time over and above their tithe. They were wonderful and amazing people — whom I love with all my heart, and still talk to frequently.

One couple who started coming about a year and a half after we started, had begun to have some financial problems. The wife was in real estate and the husband was retired. For months they went without selling any property. Soon it became such an emergency that they came to me and asked if I would pray with them and agree with them for financial breakthrough.

We prayed and agreed according to Matthew 18:18-20 (the Prayer of Agreement), they sowed their seed and within three weeks to a month they received news that they had inherited a little over $2.2 Million dollars.

God is absolutely amazing! Out of nowhere God had provided for this couple. The wife was so thankful for God's provision that she wanted to tithe on the $2.2 Million which God had obviously brought in for them. Do you know what the tithe is on 2.2 million dollars? It would have been $220,000. $20,000 over what we were believing for. It looked as if God had not only answered their prayer, but had also answered our church's prayer.

The wife called me saying how excited she was and how much she wanted to sow the tithe into our church. Trying to do the right thing, I told her to pray about it with her husband and to be led by the Holy Spirit where they were to minister the tithe. The Bible says that the tithe is the Lord's, it doesn't say that the tithe is the pastor's or the Church's.

A few weeks passed and the couple never returned to church. In fact, we didn't see or hear anything from them for over a month. After about a month the wife called me and said that she had been talking to her husband about sowing the tithe from the inheritance/miracle they had received.

She said that when she tried talking to her husband about taking one tenth (the tithe) of what they had received and giving it back to God, her husband became upset and claimed that that was "their" retirement money and he didn't want to give that much money to any ministry. I explained to her that she should keep peace in here marriage and just pray that God would change his heart.

It is sad when people turn their backs on God once He blesses them, especially when He is always so faithful. We need to be careful that we don't forget who that provision came from in the first place.

That money didn't just happen to manifest by coincidence. It wasn't the byproduct of us being holy or good. IT WAS GOD'S ANSWER TO PRAYER! It was the result of God's mercy and unmerited favor on their lives.

This answer to prayer was a clear sign illustrating that ONLY GOD is worthy of our praise and glory. It was also a test to see if this couple would be willing to honor God and move forward to further His Kingdom agenda. But once they received what they had believed for—they did what most people do—they walked away from God, because they felt they no longer needed Him.

Notice the warning found in Deuteronomy 8:11-17, "[11] Beware that you do not forget the LORD your God by not keeping His commandments, His judgments, and His statutes which I command you today, [12] lest—when you have eaten and are full, and have built beautiful houses and dwell in them; [13] and when your herds and your flocks multiply, and your silver and your gold are multiplied, and all that you have is multiplied; [14] when your heart is lifted up, and you forget the LORD your God who brought you out of the land of Egypt, from the house of bondage; [15] who led you through that great and terrible wilderness, in which were fiery serpents and scorpions and thirsty land where there was no water; who brought water for you out of the flinty rock; [16] who fed you in the wilderness with manna, which your fathers did not know, that He might humble you and *that He might test you, to do you good in the end—* [17] *then you say in your heart, 'My power and the might of my hand have gained me this wealth.'*" (Emphasis Added).

This answer to prayer was not the result of anything that we had done in our own power, but it was the result of His Goodness, that they were delivered from the bondage of debt! It had clearly been the result of confident faith and trust that we placed in His Word and provision as our Source—that had enabled God to bring this couple exactly what they had believed Him for.

If people were my source and if I looked to them to meet my needs, this event could have been devastating to my faith. But God is and always has been my Source and supply for everything and I know that no matter what, He will do what He has promised in His Word—regardless of whether or not people obey Him and do what He asks them to do.

When we experience situations like this we can cry and fuss with God about it saying things like, "But God, I have done so much..." But god doesn't reward works—He rewards faith.

If I would have acted that way with this couple that would have also been "ENTITLEMENT THINKING." That couple didn't OWE ME ANYTHING! The money God had given them was theirs, not mine...It was an answer to prayer.

I had done my job which was to pray, to believe, and to agree with them to receive their miracle from God. What that couple did with the tithe on the provision God had made available to them was between them and God—it was none of my business. My business was to treat them and to love them exactly the same way I had before they had any money—and that's exactly what I did. Amen!

We see this same type of scenario played out in Genesis 14:22-23, "22 But Abram said to the king of Sodom, "I have raised my hand to the LORD, God Most High, the Possessor of heaven and earth, 23 that I will take nothing, from a thread to a sandal strap, and that I will not take anything that is yours, lest you should say, 'I have made Abram rich"

Abram didn't want this evil king to get the credit for his success. We must learn to have the same attitude Abram had. God is our Source and NO ONE else!

If we begin to look to people to supply all of our needs, then we are going to get into big trouble and start compromising our standards. Oral Roberts once said, "Whatever you compromise to keep you will eventually lose." I believe that statement with all my heart.

As I said before, God doesn't honor our works, He honors our faith. People will let you down all the time, but God never will.

Don't get discouraged when people let you down, just begin to look to God for a better door of opportunity to open up for you. Give Him praise for his unwavering faithfulness in your life and keep on trusting Him for your provision. It will surely come if you faint not.

Nobody owes you or me anything regardless of what we have done for them. The only thing that the Bible says is owed to another is the debt of love.

Remember Our God is Yahweh Yireh—The God who sees your need beforehand and therefore provides! He knows what you need way before you do and He knows how to get it to you. After all, He knows the end from the beginning—SO TRUST HIM and love everyone while you wait for your BREAKTHROUGH!!

Daily Declaration

Heavenly Father, I am so grateful that You are not only my God, my refuge, my strength, and my healing, but You are also MY SOURCE and supply for everything I will ever need or desire. Thank You for loving me and taking such good care of everything that concerns me. I AM TRULY BLESSED!

Even when people fail me, when people turn their backs and walk away from their commitments, I know that You are my faithful God. You are Yahweh Yireh—the God who sees my need before I ever realize I need it, and You faithfully provide for that need or desire because of the covenant promise that You swore to my forefathers of the faith. You are an amazing, loving, and all-powerful God. Why would I ever need to second-guess Your love and willingness to take care of me?

Even though I have gone through some difficult times and have felt betrayed by others at times, I am grateful that I can come to You and find PEACE in the midst of every storm. You are my rock and my salvation! You are my All-in-All—the One who never leaves me or forsakes me. Thank You for always being there and for letting me know that You love me with and unfailing love. I praise You Lord, with every fiber of my being. I bless Your name and testify of Your goodness to all who are in covenant relationship with You. Praise be to the God Most High—Praise be to the name of Jesus! Amen.

Day 20
Flex Your Prayer Muscles

"⁶ But when you pray, go into your [most] private room, and, closing the door, pray to your Father, Who is in secret; and your Father, Who sees in secret, will reward you in the open. ⁷ And when you pray, do not heap up phrases (multiply words, repeating the same ones over and over) as the Gentiles do, for they think they will be heard for their much speaking."

Matthew 6:6-7 (AMP)

I have found that most people believe that if they continually pray for the same thing over and over, they believe that God will finally get tired of hearing the same thing and finally answer them. It's the philosophy of a squeaky wheel gets the oil. But God is not impressed with rituals—He's impressed by faith!

In Jeremiah 29:11 (NIV) we read, "For I know the plans I have for you," declares the LORD, "plans to prosper you and not to harm you, plans to give you hope and a future."

The Good News Translation says it like this "…Plans to bring you prosperity and not disaster, plans to bring about the future you hope for."

I like that…plans for the future I hope for. It doesn't say God's giving me a future that someone else wants to live, but one that matches my desires and His desires for me. Now that's good! It also doesn't say that I have to wait a lifetime to begin enjoying that life I've hoped for. No, I can begin living that life now if I'll put my faith to work believing Him for His promise.

The problem for many of us is that we don't understand God's character and we don't know our covenant rights as His children. God wants us Blessed! He wants us to attain our dreams and desires even more than we do. We have those desires because He meticulously crafted and wired us to be who we are. He planted those dreams deep inside of us, so that we could use our faith combined with the seeds of greatness that He planted inside of us and draw them out by His grace.

Philippians 1:6 (AMP) confirms this. In this passage Paul writes, "And I am convinced and sure of this very thing, that He Who began a good work in you will continue until the day of Jesus Christ [right up to the time of His return], developing [that good work] and perfecting and bringing it to full completion in you."

Do you see that? God is at work all the time, collaborating together with us and our faith to bring about our purpose and our desires. He's even promised to give us our desires in Psalm 37:4 saying, "Delight yourself also in the LORD, and He shall give you the desires of your heart." The real question is, "DO WE BELIEVE HIM?"

Notice Matthew 6:7 for a moment. "⁷ And when you pray, *do not heap up phrases (multiply words, repeating the same ones over and over)* as the Gentiles do, for they think they will be heard for their much speaking." The New King James Version reads, "When you pray, do not use *VAIN REPITITIONS* as the heathen do..." (Emphasis Added).

What is Jesus telling us here? He is saying, "Pray for whatever it is you need or desire, but don't pray for it over and over—otherwise you aren't praying in faith—you don't really believe that I've heard you and answered your prayer."

God is not hard of hearing! He's not preoccupied or overwhelmed with His position as God! And He's not a distant or absent God. In fact, the Bible says in Hebrews 13:5, "For He Himself has said, 'I will never leave you nor forsake you.'" The word forsake is defined as meaning: to disown, to quit on, to cast off, to abandon or desert, and to leave or reject.

God is not in the business of making promises to us and then ditching us or leaving us to fend for ourselves. When we pray we are to pray in faith and believe that what we have prayed is ours—from that moment forward.

Mark 11:23-24 explains, "²³ For assuredly, I [Jesus] say to you, whoever says to this mountain, 'Be removed and be cast into the sea,' and does not doubt in his heart, but believes that those things he says will be done, he will have whatever he says. ²⁴ *Therefore I say to you, whatever things you ask when you pray, believe that you receive them, and you will have them.*" (Emphasis Added).

When are we going to start believing we've received whatever it is that we have prayed for? Do we believe once we see it? Do we believe it's ours a week or two after we've prayed? Do we start believing that we have it after we have prayed for that same thing over and over and have met our 500ᵗʰ prayer quota? No! We believe we have it the instant that we pray for it.

When we begin praying bold, faith-filled prayers like that, Jesus said, "…YOU WILL HAVE THEM." Them what? Them things you prayed for. It might not be good English, but it's still true.

Does that mean PRESTO! God is going to do some sort of magic trick and our answer will instantly show up in our possession? No, God isn't into magic tricks, He's into faith!

Our answer can take one second or it could take many years to manifest, but regardless of the time it takes for us to receive it in this natural realm — our job is to believe that we receive it by faith until it shows up.

You may be asking yourself the question, *Why is it wrong to continually repeat my prayers? What did Jesus really mean when he said do not use vain repetitions or do not heap up phrases, repeating the same ones over and over?*

Jesus was telling us the same thing in Matthew Chapter 6 that He was saying in Mark 11:23-24. He was saying that once we have prayed for something; believe that it's ours that very instant. Don't go back to God the next day and pray for the same thing again. Otherwise, we aren't praying in faith. Faith takes possession of what it desires the instant faith Speaks. It is not moved by what it sees, but moved only by what it believes from the Word of God!

Did you know that Faith has a voice? It does. 2 Corinthians 4:13 declares, "And since we have the same spirit of faith, according to what is written, 'I believed and therefore I spoke,' we also believe and therefore speak."

Most of us know that faith is the critical ingredient in every prayer endeavor. In fact, Hebrews 11:6 tells us, "Without faith it is impossible to please Him [God], for he who comes to God must believe that He is, and that He is a rewarder of those who diligently seek Him."

Let me ask you an important question. Do you truly believe that God will answer **YOUR** prayers? If not, then why are you wasting your time praying for something you don't really believe you will ever receive? That seems a little ridiculous, don't you think? Why waste time doing something you never expect to receive results from doing? If you're going to pray for something then have the courage to believe for it and the determination to stick it out until you receive it—no matter how long it takes.

When Jesus told us not to pray vain repetitions was He saying that we should never bring up those prayers to Him ever again? No, it is perfectly fine to go back to God the next day or the next week, and say, "Lord, I came to you the other day and asked you to bring in finances to pay my bills. Father, I want to thank you that Your Word says in Philippians 4:19 that, 'My God will supply all of my needs according to His riches in glory by Christ Jesus.' Father, I believe Your Word, and I have received your Word as THE TRUTH for my life, and my situations.

Heavenly Father, 2 Corinthians 9:8 promises me, "God is able to make all grace abound toward me, that I, always having all sufficiency in all things, may have an abundance for every good work," Lord, I thank You right now that Your grace is working in my life and that I am abounding more and more in those things that I both need and desire. Thank You for sufficiently supplying me, not only in my finances, but in my health, in my relationships, in my love walk, and in every other area of my life. I pray all these things and I receive them as already being mine now, in Jesus name Amen," Now that is the way we are to pray. That is real faith in action.

In Isaiah 43:26 (KJV), God instructs us to put Him in remembrance of His Word. Is He telling us this because He's forgotten what He's promised? Did He forget where He put His Post It note with our prayer request on it? No! He wasn't instructing us to do this for His benefit, but for ours.

He was telling us to search His Word (the Bible) and to find the promises that He's already made to us, so that when we come to Him in prayer, we can rest in full assurance that it is His will for us to have the things we are requesting of Him.

That way, when the enemy comes and tries to convince us that we'll never receive what we've just prayed for, we can show Him the written proof in the Bible. We can show him that God has already both promised and granted our requests.

1 John 5:14-15 (AMP) says, "[14] And this is the confidence (the assurance, the privilege of boldness) which we have in Him: [we are sure] that if we ask anything (make any request) according to His will (in agreement with His own plan), He listens to and hears us. [15] And if (since) we [positively] know that He listens to us in whatever we ask, we also know [with settled and absolute knowledge] that we have [granted us as our present possessions] the requests made of Him." Now that's Good stuff!

I'd encourage you today, to begin flexing your prayer muscles. Don't continue praying for the same things day after day or month after month. God heard you the first time you prayed. If you've prayed in faith, that request is already on its way to you. When you begin feeling discouraged because you haven't yet seen what you've prayed for, begin giving God thanksgiving and praise for His answer to your prayer. Put Him in remembrance of His promises to you and you will also build yourself up in your faith at the same time.

He's already promised you that when you pray in faith you will have whatsoever you asked for. So take Him at His Word and begin expecting your answers to show up any second — Your Answer is on its way to you NOW! OUR GOD IS FAITHFUL!!!

Daily Declaration

Father, I am so grateful that I can confidently trust in Your Word. You have promised that Your covenant promises won't return void to You or to me. (See Numbers 23:19 and Isaiah 55:11). I rest in this confidence each and every time I come boldly to Your throne of grace and make my requests. Father, I receive Your love for me and I know that You have better plans for my life than I could ever imagine. You desire is to see me Blessed in every area of my life because You are a good, loving, and magnificent God. You are my daddy — the one who carries me in His arms and comforts me during the storms. I love You so much Lord. I am grateful for Jesus. I believe that I receive everything I request of You. This is more than just a bunch of wishes or selfish desires — it is a covenant thing! And together in covenant — You get the best of me and I receive the best of You. It doesn't seem like a fair trade, but I am grateful that You are pleased with this agreement even though You are getting the shorter end of the stick. I bless You Father, and pray these things in the mighty and wonderful name of Jesus, Amen.

Day 21
The Word Of Faith Which We Preach

"⁸ But what does it say? "The word is near you, in your mouth and in your heart" (that is, the word of faith which we preach): ⁹ that if you confess with your mouth the Lord Jesus and believe in your heart that God has raised Him from the dead, you will be saved. ¹⁰ For with the heart one believes unto righteousness, and with the mouth confession is made unto salvation.

Romans 10:8-10

Today I'd like to attempt to resolve some of the misunderstanding people have with the "Word of Faith Theology." You may have heard the terms: "Name it and claim it," Blab it and grab it," or "Confess it and possess it." These are all terms some people use to try to slam and discredit those who believe the Bible's promises and use their faith and their words to draw those promises to them.

But if you study it out in the Bible, you will find that at its core, Word of Faith Theology takes God at His Word and acts on what He has said. These Christians believe what God has promised to them in the Bible, they speak those promises over their lives, and they stand in confident faith trust God to do exactly what He said He would do—which is what real faith is all about. It's believing that God meant exactly what He said and then believing and obeying those things He said.

STANDING BETWEEN YOUR AMEN & HALLELUJAH

James 2:17 (AMP) tells us that, "Faith, if it does not have works (deeds and actions of obedience to back it up), by itself is destitute of power (inoperative, dead)."

When we speak the Word of God over our lives; that speech is the corresponding action of faith. In 2 Corinthians 4:13 the Apostle Paul wrote, "And since we have the same spirit of faith, according to what is written, "I believed and therefore I spoke," we also believe and therefore speak." Faith ALWAYS says what it believes and so does fear.

The Bible clearly states that, "So then faith *comes* by hearing, and hearing by the word of God." The Message Bible explains it this way, "The point is: Before you trust, you have to listen. But unless Christ's Word is preached, there's nothing to listen to." Fear, like faith comes by hearing the lies of the devil and is activated by speaking those lies, just like faith is activated by hearing and speaking the promises of God.

We call this the Word of Faith, because faith always speaks what it believes. We have already seen that above in 2 Corinthians 4:13 and faith always draws those things that were spoken, to us. Notice what 2 Corinthians 4:18 has to say about this spiritual force — faith ignores what the World is saying and leans entirely on the promises of God. "While we do not look at the things which are seen, but at the things which are not seen. For the things which are seen are temporary, but the things which are not seen are eternal."

Hebrews 11:1-2 (AMP) declares, "Now faith is the [substance, NKJV] the assurance (the confirmation, the title deed) of the things [we] hope for, being the proof of things [we] do not see and the conviction of their reality [faith perceiving as real fact what is not revealed to the [five] senses]. [2] For by [faith — trust and holy fervor born of faith] the men of old had divine testimony borne to them and obtained a good report."

When we say faith is the substance, we mean that faith is the material proof of something. Proof of what? It is the proof of what we have believed, desired, and hoped for by faith.

You see, we use the word hope incorrectly most of the time. Hope does not mean to wish for something. Hope is a confident trust that what was promised by God will be delivered to us just as He promised. So then it makes perfect sense that our hope is only found in God's Word.

Did you catch what Hebrews 11:2 said? "For by [faith— trust and holy fervor born of faith] the men of old had divine testimony borne to them and obtained a good report." Their hopes were based on God's promises and they received a GOOD REPORT because they placed their complete trust in those Bible promises.

There can only be a Good Report when something favorable happens—when God answers our prayers. But look at one last thing in this verse. Their good report was also based on their testimony—or what they had to say about their situations.

When they aligned their words with God's Word, they received the answers to their prayers. They received those answers because they mixed their faith with God's promises, trusting that He would do what He had promised. And God **_NEVER_** let them down. He won't let us down either if we respond to Him in the same way they did.

Numbers 23:19 declares, "God is not a man, that He should lie, nor a son of man, that He should repent. Has He said, and will He not do? Or has He spoken, and will He not make it good?"

You see, God cannot lie! It's impossible for Him to lie! Now people will lie to you all the time, but God who is love, will never lie to you. Therefore, when you find a promise about healing in the Bible, and you take it and declare it as being yours — confidently trusting that God will do what He has promised — then **_YOUR_** "Good Report" will be evidenced in your testimony and in the evidence of the healing which has taken place in your body.

The Word **_ALWAYS_** works regardless of our personal experience. If we don't see the results at work in our lives, then we need to examine ourselves and see if we have missed it somewhere. Maybe we've done something to stop up the Blessing of God: The Bible tells us that unforgiveness, unbelief, and not understanding the Word can lead to no results (See Mark 11:25, James 1:6-8, Matthew 13:19).

In Joel 3:10 we read, "Let the weak say, 'I am strong." Do you see that? If the weak say that they are weak, they will either remain that way or get worse. That is why the Bible says "Let the weak say I am strong! Strength is what the weak both need and desire — that's why they confess of speak strength over themselves instead of weakness.

Proverbs 18:20-21 states, "20 A man's stomach shall be satisfied from the fruit of his mouth; from the produce of his lips he shall be filled. 21 Death and life are in the power of the tongue, and those who love it will eat its fruit."

If the weak continued saying that they were weak, the fruit of repetitive negative speech, would result in the form of more weakness or even death. But by saying, "I am strong," these people are putting the covenant promises of God into operation and are creating life and strength within their bodies.

Both Faith and Fear have a voice — Life and Death have a voice, but it is up to us to choose which of these we want for ourselves (See Deuteronomy 30:19).

Whether we realize it or not Poverty and Wealth have a voice. Sadness and Joy have a voice — it is up to us to decide how we want to live. We choose these things every day through the words we speak.

If we continue to say what the world says, things like: "Crime is getting worse in my neighborhood," or "Everyone at work will probably be laid off," or maybe "Gas prices are too expensive for me," or "I'll probably never get married," then those are the exact things that will manifest in our lives.

But when we say what God says, things like: "I'm Blessed coming in and going out," "I'm more than a conqueror in Christ Jesus," "I'm healed by the stripes of Jesus, and I refuse to allow sickness and disease to operate in my body — in the mighty name of Jesus."

When we say things like, I don't care what things look like, My God supplies **_ALL_** of my needs according to His riches in glory, by Christ Jesus," "The Blessing of the Lord has made me rich, and He adds no sorrow to me or my family," "God has given me the desires of my heart because I delight myself in Him and His Word, and I have them now by faith in Jesus," and "God's mercy and His goodness follow me **_ALL_** the days of my life, because He said so." Then we will have those things manifesting in our lives.

Why? Because we have spoken what God has already spoken about us and we have released His BLESSING in our lives. We have put His promises to work for us — creating those things — It's a spiritual Law and It Works! It's not positive confession — It's Bible confession!

You see, real Bible faith isn't about us "a wishing and a hoping," that what we make-up will come to pass in our lives. Real Bible Faith is saying what God has already said about us in His Word — the **Bible** — and establishing those things as the "FINAL AUTHORITY" in our lives.

Those standards are the standards that God expects for us to enjoy as His covenant children and as joint heirs with Jesus. It was Jesus' substitutional sacrifice that has made us righteous before God and has granted us access to the promises in His Word. We aren't trying to twist God's arm or manipulate Him into doing something for us that He doesn't want to do. No! This is God's will — He said so in the Bible. How could we ever manipulate God even if we wanted to? That's ridiculous — He's God after all.

Now notice 1 Timothy 6:17, "Command those who are rich in this present age not to be haughty, nor to trust in uncertain riches but in the living God, **who gives us richly all things to enjoy.**"

God gives us material things to enjoy here in the earth, but He doesn't want those things to be a type of God in our lives. Material things are unstable and according to Matthew 19:20, moth and rust eventually make them decay and fade away.

The Good News however, is that God and His promises never fade away! They are eternal and they make the impossible possible (See 2 Corinthians 4:18). So trust in God and not in things. ALL things have been created and given to us to enjoy, but they should never replace God.

It's ok to have money — money isn't bad in itself, it's just a tool that gives us the ability to do more for the Kingdom of God and for others. When our heart is in the right place and

God is first in our lives, then we will use money to bless others and to further God's kingdom. We can even enjoy the things that money will allow us to do without it controlling us and ruling our lives.

I hope you can see now that there's nothing wrong with "The Word Of Faith," which is according to the Apostle Paul, is the combination of both speaking and believing what God has already said to us in the Bible. Have there been some kooks out there who have done corrupt things and hurt people? Yes, but you could say the same for people in any and every denomination!

Have some people gotten off track and taught doctrines that are contrary to the Bible? Yes! But when we allow the Bible to be our guide and not our pastor's personal experiences, then we are headed for the Blessing of God!

Learn to meditate and to speak the Word of God over your life with confidence. Romans 1:16 declares, "For I am not ashamed of the gospel of Christ, for it is the power of God to salvation [wholeness, safety, protection, prosperity, health and healing, etc.] for everyone who believes."

Believing is the prerequisite for salvation and salvation doesn't just refer to an eternity spent with God. Salvation also means wholeness in every facet of our lives.

In fact, according to John 1:14, Jesus is the Word who became flesh and lived among us, in order to give us His abundant life. He did this so that we could enjoy life and live BLESSED! Speak The Word and Live BLESSED — that is what God intended for _**ALL**_ of His Children! AMEN!

Daily Declaration

Father, I thank You for Your living Word. Hebrews 4:12 (AMP) declares, "12 For [the Word of God, NKJV] the Word that God speaks is alive and full of power [making it active, operative, energizing, and effective]; it is sharper than any two-edged sword, penetrating to the dividing line of the breath of life (soul) and [the immortal] spirit, and of joints and marrow [of the deepest parts of our nature], exposing and sifting and analyzing and judging the very thoughts and purposes of the heart."

Lord Your Word in my mouth has the same power as Your Word in Your mouth. You have created man in Your image to imitate You and to get Your results. (See Ephesians 5:1). I declare that I believe Your Word and I will speak it boldly, expecting to receive the promises You have ordained for my life.

I am positive that Your Word will not return void in my life and that Your Words spoken out of my mouth will change every negative circumstance into THE BLESSING. I receive Your best for my life today! I declare that I am the Blessed! I am the Healed! I am the Wealthy! And I am the Strong of the Lord — because I say what You have already said about me. I receive all You have for me today — in Jesus' name, Amen.

Day 22
All Of The Spoils Go To The Victor

"⁷ I have fought the good (worthy, honorable, and noble) fight, I have finished the race, I have kept (firmly held) the faith. ⁸ [As to what remains] henceforth there is laid up for me the [victor's] crown of righteousness [for being right with God and doing right], which the Lord, the righteous Judge, will award to me and recompense me on that [great] day—and not to me only, but also to all those who have loved and yearned for and welcomed His appearing (His return)."

2 Timothy 4:7-8 (AMP)

I love this passage of Scripture. It is an encouragement to know that I am not here by chance, that I am not here to mull around through life, agonizing over how I am going to make it, pay my bills, and try to find happiness in a sometimes chaotic and cruel world.

No, God has created us to be Champions, Victors, and More than Conquerors in Christ Jesus! And as a result, we should be eager to share the Good News of Jesus and the hope we have found in Him with others. You may not believe it, but Jesus is coming back very soon. How do I know? Just look at the world and look at what Jesus said would precede His return.

Notice what Matthew 24:3-14 says, "[3] Now as He sat on the Mount of Olives, the disciples came to Him privately, saying, "Tell us, when will these things be? And what will be the sign of Your coming, and of the end of the age?" [4] And Jesus answered and said to them: "Take heed that no one deceives you. [5] For many will come in My name, saying, 'I am the Christ,' and will deceive many. [6] And you will hear of wars and rumors of wars. See that you are not troubled; for all these things must come to pass, but the end is not yet. [7] For nation will rise against nation, and kingdom against kingdom. And there will be famines, pestilences, and earthquakes in various places. [8] All these are the beginning of sorrows. [9] "Then they will deliver you up to tribulation and kill you, and you will be hated by all nations for My name's sake. [10] And then many will be offended, will betray one another, and will hate one another. [11] Then many false prophets will rise up and deceive many. [12] And because lawlessness will abound, the love of many will grow cold. [13] But he who endures to the end shall be saved. [14] And this gospel of the kingdom will be preached in all the world as a witness to all the nations, and then the end will come."

This sounds exactly like the days you and I are living in, doesn't it? Now, I know this may sound "Churchy" to some of you, and you may be thinking, *How can I be excited about something that is going to take place sometime in the future, when I need a breakthrough in my life today?*" But the Bible tells us that your Breakthrough is right there in your mouth, waiting to be released by you.

In fact, Romans 10:8 says, "But what does it say? "The word is near you, in your mouth and in your heart" (that is, the word of faith which we preach)"

In other words, your Breakthrough is found in the Word of God—He has every answer, every opportunity you could ever hope for, and every miracle available to you this very instant! The Bible is the LIVING WORD OF GOD! It is alive and waiting for you to find its precious promises and to release them into your life by declaring them over yourself—commanding them to come to pass in your life—with YOUR VOICE! Are you willing to fight for what you want?

I'll admit that this life is often a battle—it is a fight of FAITH. There are many times when we may feel beat up and bruised, but that is not God's fault. Every time I have felt that way, it was because I failed to build myself up in the Word.

We have a responsibility to stir ourselves up in our faith. We are in a battle for our lives and the devil doesn't play fair. His goal is to steal, kill, and destroy you (See John 10:10), but you have been given the tools to overcome him and to live the VICTORIOUS LIFE which God planned for you, from the foundation of time.

2 Timothy 1:6 tells us, "Therefore I remind you to stir up the gift of God which is in you…" How do we do that? We do it by reminding ourselves that just because things may look bleak right now; that doesn't mean that they have to remain that way. We have the God given right and ability to change our circumstances by speaking His Word and standing on those promises by faith.

Revelation 12: 11 says of us, "And they overcame him by the blood of the Lamb and *by the word of their testimony…*" (Emphasis Added). You can literally Speak your way to victory as long as you are saying what God has already ordained for you in the Bible. I encourage you to begin declaring your healing, your wholeness, and victory in Jesus.

Satan is a defeated foe. Jesus defeated him on the Cross and we gained victory over him when we received the free gift of salvation—receiving Jesus as our Lord and Savior. The moment you gave your heart to the Lord, the bondage of sin, sickness, disease, and lack were destroyed forever in your life.

You no longer have to live as a slave to the Curse of sin, but instead, you can now live free from sin's effects by standing on the Word and establishing God's will (His Bible promise) over your life. Satan no longer has a legal right to put the Curse on you.

Galatians 3:13-14 (MSG) declares, "[13-14] Christ redeemed us from that self-defeating, cursed life by absorbing it completely into himself. Do you remember the Scripture that says, "Cursed is everyone who hangs on a tree?" [Deuteronomy 21:23]. That is what happened when Jesus was nailed to the cross: He became a curse, and at the same time dissolved the curse. And now, because of that, the air is cleared and we can see that Abraham's blessing is present and available for non-Jews, too. We are all able to receive God's life, his Spirit, in and with us by believing—just the way Abraham received it."

The only thing left to do after we understand our new found freedom in Jesus is to win as many souls as we can, and help those people to understand who they are in Christ.

It's time that we quit complaining about our situations and circumstances and begin to enforce God's Word in this earth. We have already been set-up to win!

Let's agree to get rid of our "stinking thinking" and to stir up the gift of faith that is on the inside of us. Let's start declaring God's precious promises out loud and be bold enough to believe that what He promised is already ours. If you don't like what you are experiencing — then change it! God's given you the authority to do so. He's already paid the price for your freedom on the Cross, He's given you His Word, the Blood, and the name of Jesus, and He's also implanted faith in your spirit man — so start using all of these things and speak your way to VICTORY.

Listen, I know that it can be a little intimidating doing something you have never done before. I know that it can be daunting to leave those things that are familiar for the things you've only dreamed of experiencing. And I also know that it can be stressful stepping out in faith when you're not sure how you're going to pay your bills, how you're going to have enough to eat, and how you're going to fulfill your daily obligations. But those worries don't change the truth of God's Word — if you want what you've never had, you've got to do what you've never done.

I'm not suggesting that you to jump into anything without a plan. I'm not encouraging you to quit your job today, hoping that God will drop something into your lap. All I am saying is: don't allow the devil to paralyze you into believing that you are a failure or that you are stuck where you are — that's a lie.

Get into the Word, seek God in prayer for the answers to your situation, and when you hear from heaven, be willing to obey and move forward in faith.

That old saying, "The definition of insanity is doing the same thing over and over and expecting different results," really is true!

You have been created to be a winner! You are more than a Conqueror in Christ Jesus! And you have fought gallantly in faith — NOW, it's time to claim your reward.

Life doesn't have to end in order to claim the victory! Claim a portion of it now, and then collect the remainder when Jesus returns!

Remember the great lineage and heritage from which you come. Remember that you were born to overcome and conqueror this world in the name and authority of Jesus.

1 John 4:4 states, "You are of God, little children, and have overcome them, because He who is in you is greater than he who is in the world." It's because of your relationship with Jesus that you have already won.

John 15:3-5 declares, "[3] You are already clean because of the Word which I have spoken to you. [4] Abide in Me, and I in you. As the branch cannot bear fruit of itself, unless it abides in the vine, neither can you, unless you abide in Me. [5] "I am the vine, you are the branches. He who abides in Me, and I in him, bears much fruit; for without Me you can do nothing."

You've got all you need to succeed and win in Jesus! Be willing to take the necessary steps once you have heard from heaven and enjoy the fruit of Victory in Jesus!

Daily Declaration

I declare that I am more than a conqueror in Christ Jesus. It is through His victory over the Curse, Sin, and Death that I have overcome. Jesus is my life. He is my Lord. And He is my Salvation. I have access to everything I will ever need or desire in Him. He loves me passionately and freely gives me everything I ask of Him.

Father, I thank You for Your Holy Spirit who lives inside of me and directs my every step. I am quick to hear, quick to obey, and quick to declare all that He speaks to me. I am a child of God and the Bible says that His sheep know His voice, and the voice of a stranger they will not follow. (See John 10:1-5). I follow Jesus and His Holy Spirit who leads me into all truth and into Victory.

I declare right now, that I have taken possession of all of the spoils of war. I have fought the Good Fight of Faith and overcome the enemy—in Jesus' name. In fact, Jesus said, "These things I have spoken to you, that in Me you may have peace. In the world you will have tribulation; but be of good cheer, I have overcome the world." (John 16:33).

I am an overcomer! I have the VICTORY NOW—in Jesus! I am a joint-heir with Christ and I share equally in all that He has. I pray these things in Jesus' precious and powerful name, Amen.

Day 23
The Battle Is The Lord's

"No weapon formed against you shall prosper, and every
tongue which rises against you in judgment you shall
condemn. This is the heritage of the servants of the LORD, and
their righteousness is from Me," says the LORD."

Isaiah 54:17

I t can be difficult to continue to walk in love when
people are attacking you. The natural or carnal thing
to do is to fight back and to try to get even. I
struggled with this for years and still struggle with it
at times. The old me — the sinful flesh that ruled my actions
before I was saved — wants to take control, to take over, and
make things right.

In fact, if I am honest, when someone tries to hurt me, I
want to hurt them back, so that they can never hurt me again.
But as born-again believers we are not supposed to be ruled
by our flesh, but by our spirit. We are to operate according to
a new set of laws. We no longer need to fight our own battles
because God fights them for us. The Battle is the Lord's and
the victory is ours. We now have a covenant relationship with
the Most High God of the universe and He doesn't put up
with people abusing His children.

2 Chronicles 20:15-17 declares, "Thus says the LORD to
you: 'Do not be afraid nor dismayed because of this great
multitude, for the battle is not yours, but God's. [16] Tomorrow

go down against them. They will surely come up by the Ascent of Ziz, and you will find them at the end of the brook before the Wilderness of Jeruel. [17] You will not need to fight in this battle. Position yourselves, stand still and see the salvation of the LORD, who is with you, O Judah and Jerusalem!' Do not fear or be dismayed; tomorrow go out against them, for the LORD is with you."

God sees an attack on you as a personal attack against Him. It doesn't matter how many people gang up against you. It doesn't matter how many lies they tell about you. It doesn't even matter if no one else believes your side of the story — You will come out the VICTOR and not the VICTIM!

You have a heritage of righteousness, a covenant of security and protection, and a mighty God who will protect you from every attack that may rise up against you.

Notice how God has promised to care for you when the enemy comes to steal, kill, and destroy you and to try to take your things. "[7] The LORD will cause your enemies who rise against you to be defeated before your face; they shall come out against you one way and flee before you seven ways. [8] "The LORD will command the Blessing on you in your storehouses and in all to which you set your hand, and He will bless you in the land which the LORD your God is giving you." (Deuteronomy 28:7-8).

Psalm 94:22-23 says, "But the LORD has been my defense, and my God the rock of my refuge. [23] He has brought on them their own iniquity, and shall cut them off in their own wickedness; the LORD our God shall cut them off."

What the enemy has been saying about you will come back on him. Deuteronomy 30:7 says, "[7] Also the LORD your God will put all these curses on your enemies and on those

Who hate you, who persecuted you."

Nahum 1:2-3 tells us, "² God is jealous, and the LORD avenges; the LORD avenges and is furious. The LORD will take vengeance on His adversaries, and He reserves wrath for His enemies; ³ The LORD is slow to anger and great in power, and will not at all acquit the wicked."

Hebrews 10:30 declares, "Vengeance is Mine, I will repay," says the Lord." It is a spiritual law that what a person sows, that is also what they will reap (Genesis 8:22; Luke 6:38; 2 Corinthians 9:6-7; Galatians 6:7). If we want to live Blessed lives we must live a life of love.

Moreover, Romans 12:18-20 instructs, "¹⁸ If it is possible, as much as depends on you, live peaceably with all men. ¹⁹ Beloved, do not avenge yourselves, but rather give place to wrath; for it is written, "Vengeance is Mine, I will repay," says the Lord. ²⁰ Therefore "If your enemy is hungry, feed him; if he is thirsty, give him a drink; for in so doing you will heap coals of fire on his head."

Now notice what Jesus says in Matthew 5:43-45, "⁴³ You have heard that it was said, 'You shall love your neighbor and hate your enemy.' ⁴⁴ But I say to you, love your enemies, bless those who curse you, do good to those who hate you, and pray for those who spitefully use you and persecute you, ⁴⁵ that you may be sons of your Father in heaven; for He makes His sun rise on the evil and on the good, and sends rain on the just and on the unjust."

One of the first promises God gave to Abraham after cutting the covenant with him is found in Genesis 12:3, "I will bless those who bless you, and I will curse him who curses you; and in you all the families of the earth shall be blessed."

We find this again in Genesis 27:29 where God says, "...Cursed be everyone who curses you, and blessed be those who bless you!"

There is no need for a Christian to feel like he/she must get even when people do rotten things to them. To put it in today's vernacular, "God's got your back." He won't allow the enemy to harm you when you are walking in love and walking in obedience to His Word.

It may look like your losing ground when you're walking in love and not retaliating towards those who have hurt you, but cheer up! Pray for your adversaries to receive Jesus and then rest in faith knowing that your battle is not a physical one of flesh and blood, but a spiritual battle against Satan and his demons.

The people who are attacking you are being used like pawns and the devil is trying to steal your joy. As Jerry Savelle has so eloquently stated, "If the Satan can't steal your joy — he can't keep your goods." This attack against you is just an attempt to get you to lash out in strife. If you fall for it — you open yourself up to his schemes and give him a foothold in your life.

Don't fall for it! Don't allow the devil to move you from the Blessing over into the Curse! Instead, walk in love and win the battle. "[21] If your enemy is hungry, give him bread to eat; and if he is thirsty, give him water to drink; [22] For so you will heap coals of fire on his head, and the LORD will reward you." (Proverbs 25:21-22).

REMEMBER — THE BATTLE IS THE LORD'S BUT THE VICTORY IS YOURS — PRAISE GOD!

Daily Declaration

I declare that I walk in the continual Blessing of God because I walk in love and avoid strife. I refuse to fall for the enemy's tactics, but instead, I guard my heart and my mind diligently, by meditating on God's Word daily.

Lord, help me to recognize when the enemy is trying to move me through emotional or physical attacks. Protect me Father, and remind me that You are my shelter, my vindicator, and the one who fights for me.

I am not concerned about my reputation, but I am concerned with obeying Your commands. I know that if I am not moved by Satan's sly strategies, then he can't have any access into my life.

I charge my angels to go before me, behind me, and to encompass me as a shield of protection. (See Psalm 5:12). I declare that I will not act or speak anything but those things that will build people up and draw them to Jesus.

I crucify my flesh and command it to submit to the Lord Jesus, trusting that He will bring me out victorious in every battle I face.

Just as You have declared in Your Word Father, "24 Though he[the righteous man] fall, he shall not be utterly cast down; for the LORD upholds him with His hand. 25 I have been young, and now am old; yet I have not seen the righteous forsaken, nor his descendants begging bread." (Psalm 37:24-25).

I am the righteousness of God in Christ and I pray these things in the mighty name of Jesus, Amen!

Day 24
Joy Is The Result Of Who You Know & What You've Received By Faith

"² My brethren, count it all joy when ye fall into divers
temptations; ³ Knowing this, that the trying of your faith
worketh patience.⁴ But let patience have her perfect work, that
ye may be perfect and entire, wanting nothing."

James 1:2-4 (KJV)

Many people misinterpret this passage by
suggesting that James was instructing Christians
to believe that suffering is part of the Christian
faith and that those who suffer bring glory to
God. But there is no place in Scripture that we find any
indication of sickness, pain, and suffering bringing God glory.
In fact we find the opposite.

Jesus did tell us, "In the world you will have
tribulation; but be of good cheer, I have overcome the world."
(John 16:33).

The Amplified Bible explains this further by stating, "In
the world you have tribulation and trials and distress and
frustration; but be of good cheer [take courage; be confident,
certain, undaunted]! For I have overcome the world. *[I have
deprived it of power to harm you and have conquered it for
you.]*" (Emphasis Added).

Jesus has totally destroyed and disarmed the enemy's
power against us. He has rescued us from the power of the
Curse and freed us from its bondage and lasting effects.

Anyone who would suggest that James was instructing his brothers and sisters in Christ to understand suffering as a gift from God, has a screw loose! Simply put—t hat is bad theology! If that were true, it would make God an abusive Father—which He is not!

Yet there are millions of Christians who have come to believe these kinds of things about God. They have been duped into believing that God uses sickness, harm, and even death, to teach us to be more Christ-like.

I have even heard some people say unscriptural things like, "I'm just suffering for Jesus, but I wouldn't change it for the world." Oh Hooey! You and I can't suffer for Jesus—He was perfect—and we aren't! Why would He want you to suffer for Him in the first place? Jesus doesn't need a Savior— you and I do!

If these people enjoy suffering so much, then why are they always complaining about how unfair life is? Why do they waste time taking medication and visiting doctors? Why don't they just man up and suffer with their problems and quit trying to alleviate the pain and the problems their facing?

I'll tell you why—it's because they are insincere! Their empty words are a futile attempt to portray themselves as being holy. Somewhere along the way (probably dating back to the Desert Fathers), Satan convinced man that he could add his works to the WORK of the Cross—but that's a lie! There is ***ABOSOLUTELY NOTHING,*** that you or I can add to the finished work of the Cross!

Notice what Romans 5:3-5 says, "We also glory in tribulations, knowing that tribulation produces perseverance; [4] and perseverance, character; and character, hope. [5] Now hope does not disappoint, because the love of God has been poured out in our hearts by the Holy Spirit who was given to us."

Paul is saying the exact same thing James said above. He is telling us that when we go through difficult times, we have a hope which produces joy inside of us, in spite of the pain and suffering we are experiencing in the flesh. That hope and joy come from knowing in whom we've put our trust. It is a joy that is born out of recognizing and confidently trusting in our Deliverer — Jesus!

Look at what 2 Timothy 1:10-12 (NLT) says, "[10] And now He [God] has made all of this plain to us by the appearing of Christ Jesus, our Savior. He broke the power of death and illuminated the way to life and immortality through the Good News. [11] And God chose me to be a preacher, an apostle, and a teacher of this Good News. [12] That is why I am suffering here in prison. But I am not ashamed of it, for I know the one in whom I trust, and I am sure that he is able to guard what I have entrusted to him until the day of his return."

The Message Bible explains it this way, "[8-10] So don't be embarrassed to speak up for our Master or for me, his prisoner. Take your share of suffering for the Message along with the rest of us. We can only keep on going, after all, by the power of God, who first saved us and then called us to this holy work. We had nothing to do with it. It was all his idea, a gift prepared for us in Jesus long before we knew anything about it. But we know it now. Since the appearance of our Savior, nothing could be plainer: death defeated, life vindicated in a steady blaze of light, all through the work of Jesus. [11-12] This is the Message I've been set apart to proclaim as preacher, emissary, and teacher. It's also the cause of all this trouble I'm in. But I have no regrets. I couldn't be more sure of my ground — the One I've trusted in can take care of what he's trusted me to do right to the end.

Psalm 18:1-6 declares, "I will love You, O LORD, my strength. ² The LORD is my rock and my fortress and my deliverer; my God, my strength, in whom I will trust; my shield and the horn of my salvation, my stronghold. ³ I will call upon the LORD, who is worthy to be praised; so shall I be saved from my enemies. ⁴ The pangs of death surrounded me, and the floods of ungodliness made me afraid. ⁵ The sorrows of Sheol surrounded me; the snares of death confronted me. ⁶ In my distress I called upon the LORD, and cried out to my God; He heard my voice from His temple, and my cry came before Him, even to His ears."

And in 1 Corinthians 10:13 we are encouraged, "No temptation has overtaken you except such as is common to man; but God is faithful, who will not allow you to be tempted beyond what you are able, but with the temptation will also make the way of escape, that you may be able to bear it."

That doesn't mean that God keeps packing bad stuff on us brick by brick. No, that means that when the devil comes to steal, kill, and destroy everything we have, because he hates us, God won't allow him to take us out.

The only way Satan can kill you is if you allow him to. No, God has got your back. He is your Salvation — He is *El Shaddai* — the God who is whatever you need Him to be — Deliverer, Protector, Healer, Financier, Shelter, Friend, Loving Father, Husband — whatever it is you need!

Yes, James 1:2 instructs us to be joyful when we experience trouble because we have a rescuer waiting in the wings to pull us out of our mess and out of the traps we have fallen into while being deceived by the devil.

An important part of our rescue however, is found in verse 3; "Knowing this, that the trying of your faith worketh patience."

The words worketh patience, can be translated as being: to employ patience or to employ endurance. When you are in a race or a fight, endurance is crucial. If you tire out to quickly, you'll lose. Your opponent will pass you by or knock you out.

James is explaining that we need to train and become skillful with the Word of God and the weapons of our warfare (See Ephesians 6). All of those weapons will help us to grow stronger in our faith and to overcome Satan, each time we encounter him.

Think about it in these terms. Do you remember the first time you started training at the gym? At first it was uncomfortable, you were weak, and your muscles were sore. But after continued exposure to that environment, you built up endurance and strength.

The same is true with spiritual things. What at first seemed difficult and often took months to overcome, has now become second nature. You have learned how to persevere and conquer.

That is why Hebrews 10:35-36 encourages us saying, "[35]Therefore do not cast away your confidence, which has great reward. [36] For you have need of endurance, so that after you have done the will of God, you may receive the promise."

Verse 4; offers us more clarity. "[4] But let patience have her perfect work, that ye may be perfect and entire, wanting nothing."

Patience and perseverance is a must when it comes to faith. In fact, patience and confident trust in God, regardless of what things look like in the natural realm, is the "work of faith." It's what James was referring to when he said, " So also faith, if it does not have works (deeds and actions of obedience to back it up), by itself is destitute of power (inoperative, dead)." (James 2:17, AMP).

Unfortunately, we have become a society with drive-thru mentality. Some things take longer than 60 seconds to accomplish. Most millionaires spent years working to gain their wealth. Your education and degree came as a result of time spent and perseverance in actions. Good relationships take time and practice.

Some people may try to tell you that James was suggesting in James 1:2-4, that we need to be patient and put up with the Devil's garbage when we experience problems, because that's just God's way of teaching us how to be holy— BUT DON"T BELIEVE THEM!

God is the BLESSER not the CURSER. He is LOVE not an ABUSER!

The next time you encounter a trial consider it joy— I'm not talking about the problem, but I'm talking about the fact that God has already made you victorious even before you begin the fight!

You can be joyful knowing that Jesus and your angels are standing in front and all around you protecting you from Satan's harm. In fact they are putting the hurt on the devil and his posse. You can be joyful knowing that once the dust settles you'll come out without a scratch on you and you will be completely satisfied! God Is Good— All The Time! AMEN!

Daily Declaration

Father, I give You praise for my victory in advance of the battle. You are my amazing God who goes before me to fight the battle, to protect me in the midst of the storm, and to bring me out victoriously and unscathed. With You as my God who dare stand against me?

I am overwhelmed by Your unfailing love and for the constant acts of favor that You perform in my life. I don't deserve any of those things, yet You still flood me with Your Blessing! You truly are amazing!

Father, today I pray for my family, for my co-workers, for my friends, and for those who don't yet know You. Lord, I ask You to open up a door for me to share a glimmer of Your goodness with each and every one of them. I want the entire world to know how AWESOME You are.

I also pray for my country and ask you to put a hedge of protection around it. I break Satan's power over my nation's leadership. I pray for all of those in governmental power to recognize Your Authority and to humble themselves before You—making You their God and obeying Your commands. I speak peace and healing to the nations of this world! I bind the devil and his plot to destroy Israel—in the mighty name of Jesus! I render Satan, and those who oppose Israel and what she stands for, harmless and ineffective in their attacks against her. I pray for the peace of Jerusalem—In Jesus' name, Amen!

Day 25
Can't Keep A Righteous Man Down!

"No matter how many times you trip them up, God-loyal people don't stay down long; soon they're up on their feet, while the wicked end up flat on their faces."

Proverbs 24:16 (MSG)

D o you remember the commercial for the 1970's toys the Weeble Wobbles? The slogan was, "Weebles Wobble, but they don't fall down." I used to love those things. If you're not familiar with them, Weebles were egg shaped toys that were made to look like people and animals.

Inside, was a weight that would keep them standing upright, no matter how they were dropped. If you rolled them around, they would wobble from side to side, but they would always return to an upright position.

That is exactly what this verse is saying about God's covenant children. What the enemy meant for evil, God will turn and use it for good (See Genesis 50:20). The enemy may be trying to take you out, he way be trying to make you wobble and lose your composure, but because you have a covenant with God, he can't take you out or do you any lasting harm unless you allow him to.

I remember when I first gave my heart to the Lord. Back then, I believed that God was a BIG GOD, but I also thought that the devil was a big devil. I didn't know that Satan was such a fraud. I didn't know that he isn't as big as he portrays himself to be.

I want you to know here and now—that God and Satan not equal in their power. Satan has used the media to build himself up and has tried to convince people that he is a bigger deal than he really is. God is so much more powerful than the devil and so are you.

In fact, God has given you authority and dominion over the enemy. He has given you the name of Jesus, to which Satan must bow his knee.

Every time I think about the devil now, which is very little, I think of the movie, *The Wizard of OZ*. Do you remember when Dorothy, the Tin Man, the Scarecrow, and the Cowardly Lion all went to visit the famous Wizard? There was a huge screen, eerie green smoke, and big booming speakers that made the Wizard of Oz seem larger than life.

He wanted everyone to believe that he was extremely powerful. But when Toto (Dorothy's dog) pulled back the curtain, he was really a little shrimp of a man, with no real power of his own.

The same is true about the devil. The only authority he has is the power that we give to him through our sin, our fear, and our words, but he has no real authority over Christians. He does however, have authority over those who haven't made Jesus the Lord and Savior of their lives—in fact, he can legally kill take you out if you're not saved—because sin has made Satan the god of those who haven't received Jesus as their Savior.

Psalm 34 is one of my most favorite passages of Scripture. Whenever I feel defeated or backed up against the wall, this passage reminds me of God's goodness and it builds up my faith.

"[4] I sought the LORD, and He heard me, and delivered me from all my fears. [5] They [His covenant children] looked to Him and were radiant, and their faces were not ashamed. [6] This poor man cried out, and the LORD heard him, and saved him out of all his troubles. [7] The angel of the LORD encamps all around those who fear Him [worshipfully respect and honor Him as their God], and delivers them." (Psalm 34:4-7).

Psalm 34:17, 19-22 continues by declaring, "[17] The righteous cry out, and the LORD hears, and delivers them out of all their troubles...[19] Many are the afflictions of the righteous, but the LORD delivers him out of them all. [20] He guards all his bones; not one of them is broken. [21] Evil shall slay the wicked, and those who hate the righteous shall be condemned. [22] The LORD redeems the soul of His servants, and none of those who trust in Him shall be condemned."

Those are amazing promises, but God doesn't stop there. Micah 7:8 says, "Do not rejoice over me, my enemy; When I fall, I will arise; when I sit in darkness, The LORD will be a light to me."

In other words, when you and I fall down, we're not meant to stay down long. In fact, just like a Weeble Wobble we are to pop right back up on our feet—singing our song of VICTORY and praising our FAITHFUL God.

You and I weren't created to lie on the ground and suck dirt, but the Devil was! Do you remember the Garden of Eden? It was the Serpent who was cursed for coming into the Garden illegally and deceiving Adam and Eve. He was the one God said was cursed to slither around on his belly for all eternity.

In Psalm 37:23-24 we read, "The steps of a good man are ordered by the LORD, and He delights in his way. [24] Though he fall, he shall not be utterly cast down; for the LORD upholds him with His hand."

Psalm 5:11-12 tells us, "[11] But let all those rejoice who put their trust in You; let them ever shout for joy, because You defend them; let those also who love Your name be joyful in You. [12] For You, O LORD, will bless the righteous; with favor You will surround him as with a shield." God's unmerited favor, His Blessing surrounds those who belong to Him.

Speaking of God's saving power, Job 5:19 declares, "He shall deliver you in six troubles, yes, in seven no evil shall touch you."

Do you see that? God is there for us each and every time we need Him. It doesn't matter how many times the enemy comes after us to do us harm, God never sleeps, He never slumbers, He is always on patrol, keeping His children safe and out of sin's grasp.

We must all remember what Proverbs 24:16 (MSG) says about God's covenant children, "No matter how many times [the enemy tries to] trip them up, God-loyal people don't stay down long; soon they're up on their feet, while the wicked end up flat on their faces."

It's not productive or healthy to give our attention to the problems we face in life, instead, we have been called to look to our God, to dust the dust off of our hands, and stand up straight waiting for our vindication and triumph.

Psalm 121 1-8 says it the best, "I will lift up my eyes to the hills — from whence comes my help? [2] My help comes from the LORD, Who made heaven and earth. [3] He will not allow your foot to be moved; He who keeps you will not slumber.[4] Behold, He who keeps Israel shall neither slumber nor sleep. [5] The LORD is your keeper; The LORD is your shade at your right hand. [6] The sun shall not strike you by day, nor the moon by night. [7] The LORD shall preserve you from all evil; He shall preserve your soul. [8] The LORD shall preserve your going out and your coming in from this time forth, and even forevermore."

You may feel a little unstable at times. You may feel like a Weeble Wobble tipping forward and backwards, but remember how you were created — You were created to stand and created for VICTORY in JESUS!

No matter what attacks come your way, you have a promise that you will be triumphant. It's not the start of the race that matters, what matters is who is standing in the Winner's Circle after the race has finished.

When the dust settles and medals are handed out — only those who have made Jesus their Lord, will receive their victor's crown. And the wicked will be lying flat on their faces and reeling from the beating they've taken from messing with God's chosen people — Praise God! You're On The Winning Team!

Daily Declaration

I declare that just like a Weeble Wobble—When I fall, I shall arise! (See Micah 7:8) Devil, you can't keep this righteous man/woman down—in the name of Jesus! The Lord is my strength and my salvation whom shall I fear (See Psalm 27:1). If God is for me, who dare stand against me? (See Romans 8:31). I am the Righteousness of God in Christ Jesus. (2 Corinthians 5:21). No weapon formed against me shall prosper and every tongue that rises against me in judgment, I shall condemn in Jesus' name (Isaiah 54:17). I am more than a conqueror in Christ Jesus! That means I win every battle I come up against. (See Romans 8:37).

Thank You Father, for raising me up in Jesus and for giving me new life in Him—I am a new creation in Christ, the old has passed away, behold ALL [every part of me] has become new—the old me died on the Cross with Jesus—Hallelujah!!! (See 2 Corinthians 5:17). I am alive. I am FREE. I am Blessed and empowered to live the abundant life (a life specifically designed for me by God), a life that He knew I would love and enjoy. (See John 10:10, AMP). I love You Jesus! And I pray these things in Your precious name Jesus—AMEN!

Day 26
God Is A Superabundant, More Than Enough, Too Much God!

"[20] Now to Him Who, by (in consequence of) the [action of His] power that is at work within us, is able to [carry out His purpose and] do superabundantly, far over *and* above all that we [dare] ask or think [infinitely beyond our highest prayers, desires, thoughts, hopes, or dreams] — [21] To Him be glory in the church and in Christ Jesus throughout all generations forever and ever. Amen (so be it)."

Ephesians 3:20-21 (AMP)

God is an awesome, more than enough, too much God. In fact Jesse Duplantis, one of my heroes wrote a book with that exact title. Our God is the God of ABUNDANCE. He has never been a "Penny Pincher," a "Cheap Skate,", or the least bit stingy, because He is the God of Love and He has an abundant supply of everything we could ever desire.

In fact, our God is always over the top, more than enough, beyond measure, a cup running over kind of God. Why? Is it because He is wasteful? Is it because He doesn't realize when enough is enough?

No, it's because He wants us to understand that He is our Source and that there's NOTHING that He cannot provide for His covenant children. In fact, God wants to lavish His love upon us so much that He does things that are so much bigger than we could ever imagine. In fact God has created us to DREAM BIG just like Him, but RELIGION has taught us that doing things in excellence and believing for the best is a waste of God's resources--but that's just not true! Think about it for a minute—if those things are being used to Bless people, to change their lives for the better, and for expanding the Kingdom—then God is not opposed to you having them..

Proverbs 10:22 (AMP) says, "The blessing of the Lord—it makes [truly] rich, and He adds no sorrow with it [neither does toiling increase it]." Outside of Him, nothing we do in our own strength will work like it does when we tap into His power and His anointing.

Notice what Psalm 23:1, 5-6 says, "¹The LORD is my shepherd; I shall not want…⁵You prepare a table before me in the presence of my enemies; You anoint my head with oil; my cup runs over. ⁶Surely goodness and mercy shall follow me all the days of my life. And I will dwell in the house of the LORD forever. "

That first verse has been taught incorrectly for centuries. Satan's lies have been perpetuated for so long that people have begun to believe that it's evil to have any material wealth. They've been conned into feeling guilty for having desires, dreams, and aspirations for success and enjoying life. But that isn't what God was saying through the Psalmist.

The idea He was trying to convey to His covenant children is that God is the Good Shepherd! And as the Good Shepherd—He takes care of all the needs and desires of His flock. He makes sure His sheep are well fed, well rested, protected, and that they have everything they could ever desire. He is so good to them that there is nothing else that they could ever want because they already have it.

Psalm 37:4 reminds us of this same truth, "Delight yourself also in the LORD, and He shall give you the desires of your heart."

God wants us to have the things we both need and desire, but He doesn't want those things having us! He doesn't want things to take His place as God in our lives. It's really all about our hearts and putting God first place in our lives. Do we truly love God, or are we just using Him to get things?

If we look back at Psalm 23:5 we read, "⁵You prepare a table before me in the presence of my enemies; You anoint my head with oil; my cup runs over."

People often get mad and accuse ministers of wasting God's resources when they see them having nice cars, nice houses, or nice toys. Why? Because they automatically start thinking that those things came as a result of cheating people out of their money and spending it on themselves. NO! IT ALL CAME AS A RESULT OF GOD'S BLESSING!

Sure, there are some crooks in every profession who cheat, steal, and destroy people's lives, but that is a result of who they are connected to — the devil.

The reason Psalm 23:5 says my cup runs over, is because the Blessing is an unlimited supply and God shares all He has with His loved ones — That is simply His character.

2 Corinthians 9:8 expresses this same sentiment, "And God is able to make all grace abound toward you, that you, always having all sufficiency **_IN ALL THINGS_**, may have abundance for every good work." (EMPHASIS ADDED).

I want YOU to know that... God is able! In fact, we could stop right there and I'd feel like we'd gone to church today! Our God is ABLE to do Exceeding, Abundantly, Above

ALL we could ever think or imagine!!! (See Ephesians 3:20, AMP). Whenever things look impossible, just remember that God is able. When things look dark and like they'll never ever get better, just remember that God is able!

The good news is that 2 Corinthians 9:8 doesn't stop there—it continues by saying—He is able to: make all grace abound toward you, that you, always having all sufficiency in all things, may have an abundance for every good work.

I like the Amplified version even better, "And God is able to make all grace (every favor and earthly blessing) come to you in abundance, so that you may always and under all circumstances and whatever the need be self-sufficient [possessing enough to require no aid or support and furnished in abundance for every good work and charitable donation]."

But I'd be cheating you if I didn't point out that there is a condition to this promise—You Must be a sower in order to qualify.

God has plenty of whatever you need. He is not limited by recession, world currency issues, politics, war, gas prices, none of that stuff has ever knocked Him of His throne.

Like Jesse Duplantis says, God has never turned to Jesus and said, "Jesus, it looks pretty rough down there on earth, I think we better sell the Pearly Gates, if We're going to make it through this one." No, if God needs more He just speaks it into existence. Did you know that you and I are expected to do the same thing?

Ephesians 5:1 tells us, "Therefore be imitators of God as dear children." Whenever you and I need or desire something, we are to go to the Word of God and find the promise for the provision of that "thing," in the Bible.

He's already said that it is ours, but we need the proof that it belongs to us according to His will (the Bible), in order to build ourselves up and strengthen our confidence in the truth that it's His will for us to have it. Once we have the Scriptural evidence then the next step is to start speaking those Bible promises over our circumstances, believing that you have them the instant we pray for them.

When we have the courage to act on what the Bible says, we will always have some people who will say, "Well you're just trying to act like God. Who do you think you are?"

My answer is always, "I am the righteousness of God in Christ. I am a joint heir with Jesus, sharing in EVERYTHING He has just as He planned for me to. Didn't Ephesians 5:1 just tell us to act like God? Therefore, if I'm supposed to mimic God, then I'm supposed to do what He did. If my actions are "STRANGE" to you, then who are you acting like by remaining in unbelief and doubt?"

That's what Ephesians 3:20 (AMP) is telling us, "Now to Him Who, by (in consequence of) the [action of His] power that is at work within us, is able to [carry out His purpose and] do superabundantly, far over and above all that we [dare] ask or think [infinitely beyond our highest prayers, desires, thoughts, hopes, or dreams]."

We have "IT" IN US, because HE is IN US! We have His Spirit living, working, and operating inside of us. Be bold and dare to DREAM and to LIVE BIG — it's what God intended from the foundation of the earth! HALLELUJAH!

God wants to do so much more in our lives than we have ever imagined. He has deposited within us, His ability and His power, so that we can succeed. He is not like the world portrays Him to be.

He is concerned with your needs, your desires, and your dreams, because He is passionately in love with you. He is the one who gave you those unique passions, in order to accomplish His purpose in you and in this world. It is crazy to think that God would place those dreams, talents, and desires inside of us and then never allow us the opportunity or resources to utilize them.

No, the devil is sly. He wants us to think that God is unfair, stingy, and all about rules and keeping us from having any fun, but in reality, that is just a projection of himself.

God is love and love never fails. God is *El Shaddai* — Almighty God — The God of More Than Enough. Nothing is too big or too hard for Him to accomplish through those who will yield themselves to Him.

Jesus gave us a glimpse into that truth in John 14:12-13, when He said, "[12] Most assuredly, I say to you, he who believes in Me, the works that I do he will do also; and greater works than these he will do, because I go to My Father. [13] And whatever you ask in My name, that I will do, that the Father may be glorified in the Son."

God is not put off by you asking for things. He knows that you have needs, desires, and dreams (Matthew 6:32). He is glorified when we come to Him asking Him for our miracles. He enjoys being our Source and our Supply for everything. He created the system to work that way, but society has been deceived by the devil, into believing that it is just selfish excess.

In reality it is man recognizing his need for a God who is intimately aware of his needs, desires, and dreams. And it is about a God who so thoroughly wants to show up and to show out on our behalf, because He is overflowing in love for us.

Dare to THINK BIG, dare to DREAM BIG, and dare to ASK BIG PRAYERS. If you do, you will see God do more than you could ever imagine. If You are a born-again believer in Jesus, you have everything you need deposited on inside of you. He's on the inside of you — now it's time to give birth to your dreams and to experience the power of our SUPERABUDANT, MORE THAN ENOUGH, TOO MUCH GOD — Hallelujah — God is good!!!

Daily Declaration

Thank You Lord for supplying ALL of my needs and for showing up every single time I call out to You for help. You are my SUPERABUNDANT, MORE THAN ENOUGH, TOO MUCH GOD! I am ***ALWAYS*** amazed by Your goodness in my life.

I am thankful that I can trust You in the midst of the turmoil that tries to come my way. There is NOTHING that is BIGGER or MORE POWERFUL than You! Not only have You defeated the enemy's attacks against me, but You have sheltered me in Your love and surrounded me with Your FAVOR, INCREASE, and PROMOTION!

I declare that I am a magnet to Your Blessing Lord! Your Blessing ALWAYS finds me and overtakes me, because I obey Your commands and because I am a sower. Your Bible promises me that I will reap what I sow, but the good news is I can't out give You Lord.

2 Corinthians 8:9 (AMP) says about me, "For you are becoming progressively acquainted with and recognizing more strongly and clearly the grace of our Lord Jesus Christ (His kindness, His gracious generosity, His undeserved favor and spiritual blessing), [in] that though He was [so very] rich, yet for your sakes He became [so very] poor, in order that by His poverty you might become enriched (abundantly supplied)."

Thank You for being so good to me — I bless Your holy name and receive Your gifts in Jesus' mighty name — Amen.

Day 27
The Sun Of Righteousness Will Rise With Healing In His Wings

"But for you who fear my name, the Sun of Righteousness will rise with healing in his wings. And you will go free, leaping with joy like calves let out to pasture."

Malachi 4:2 (NLT)

I t may not be obvious to everyone reading Malachi Chapter 4, but the Sun of Righteousness is referring to the person of Jesus, who is also the light of God's goodness and the One who has brought deliverance into this fallen world. His light is as bright as the sun and He is the symbol and the manifested promise of HOPE, DELIVERANCE, and HEALING for all mankind.

In Malachi 4:2, we read that Jesus will rise with healing in His wings. The word wings in Malachi 4:2, comes from the Hebrew word *kanaph*, which means: wing, extremity, corner, edge, or covering. Jewish Rabbi's would wear their prayer shawls (*tallit*), which were used as a kind of covering while they prayed (a prayer closet, if you will).

On each of the four outer edges of these prayer shawls, were little knotted strings that hung down from the corners. Each knot represented one of the 613 *Mitzvot* (the sacred Jewish commandments or laws), which are found in the Jewish Torah. These little knotted strings are called *tzitzit* or *tzitziot*, in Hebrew.

When the rabbis and devout Jews would cover themselves with their prayer shawls to commence their prayers, the ends of the shawl would look similar to the wings of a large bird. Therefore, the Jewish believers living during Jesus' time; were very familiar with the concept of the prayer shawl representing wings. They understood that Malachi 4:2 was a prophecy testifying to the coming Messiah, who would come to earth with supreme power, authority, dominion, and anointing to heal all who were oppressed of the devil and held captive by their sin.

In Isaiah 10:27 we learn about the yoke destroying burden removing anointing of God. "It shall come to pass in that day that his burden [Satan's Curse of sin] will be taken away from your shoulder, and his yoke from your neck, and the yoke will be destroyed because of the anointing oil [Jesus]."

It is the anointing of Jesus, His authority and dominion over sin, sickness, and death which destroys the yoke of the devil.

Notice Mark 5:25-30, "[25] Now a certain woman had a flow of blood for twelve years, [26] and had suffered many things from many physicians. She had spent all that she had and was no better, but rather grew worse. [27] When she heard about Jesus, she came behind Him in the crowd and touched His garment. [28] For she said, "If only I may touch His clothes [wings, *tzitzit*], I shall be made well." [29] Immediately the fountain of her blood was dried up, and she felt in her body that she was healed of the affliction. [30] And Jesus, immediately knowing in Himself that power had gone out of Him, turned around in the crowd and said, "Who touched My clothes?"

Mark 3:9-10, illustrates that the people who lived during Jesus' time clearly understood and were looking forward to the coming of Messiah who would be a deliverer and heal all who had faith to believe. "[9] So He told His disciples that a small boat should be kept ready for Him because of the multitude, lest they should crush Him. [10] For He healed many, so that as many as had afflictions pressed about Him to touch Him. [11] And the unclean spirits, whenever they saw Him, fell down before Him and cried out, saying, "You are the Son of God."

Matthew 14:34-36 says, "[34] When they had crossed over, they came to the land of Gennesaret. [35] And when the men of that place recognized Him, they sent out into all that surrounding region, brought to Him all who were sick, [36] and begged Him that they might only touch the hem [the *tzitzit*], of His garment. And as many as touched it were made perfectly well."

In essence, just like the Sun brings forth natural light to illuminate the way, the Son of God brings forth Spiritual Light to illuminate the way through spiritual darkness. We call this Spiritual Light — Righteousness.

Jesus was the Light who would dispel the darkness of this world. His righteousness is as bright as the Sun. He is literally the Son of Righteous and there are numerous Scriptures which testify to His glory and majesty.

Psalm 84:11-12 declares, "For the LORD God is a sun and shield; the LORD will give grace and glory; no good thing will He withhold from those who walk uprightly. [12] O LORD of hosts, blessed is the man who trusts in You!"

Isaiah 58:8-9 says, "8Then your light shall break forth like the morning, your healing shall spring forth speedily, and your righteousness shall go before you; the glory of the LORD shall be your rear guard. 9Then you shall call, and the LORD will answer; you shall cry, and He will say, 'Here I am.'"

Matthew 4:16-17 tells us "16The people who sat in darkness have seen a great light, and upon those who sat in the region and shadow of death, Light has dawned." 17From that time Jesus began to preach and to say, "Repent, for the kingdom of heaven is at hand."

2 Corinthians 4:6 confirms, "For it is the God who commanded light to shine out of darkness, who has shone in our hearts to give the light of the knowledge of the glory of God in the face of Jesus Christ."

Even Jesus Himself, testified to being the Light. In John 8:12 He says, "I am the light of the world. He who follows Me shall not walk in darkness, but have the light of life."

And in John 12:46 Jesus said, "I have come as a light into the world, that whoever believes in Me should not abide in darkness."

Once we recognize the fact that Jesus came as the Sun of Righteousness, as the Light of the world, with healing in His wings, then we begin to understand that healing belongs to _**ALL**_ of us, who are in Christ.

We begin to understand that Jesus did not die for Himself, He didn't need a Savior; we did! We begin to understand that healing was a vital part of what Jesus died to provide for us. He conquered sin once and for all!

Satan was ultimately defeated on the cross because Jesus was a sinless and innocent man. Satan illegally crucified Him, thereby breaking the law of Heaven. The devil, illegally overstepped his authority, and committed a crime against an innocent man—Jesus.

Yet in reality, Jesus gave Himself willingly, as a substitute for all mankind. That is how we have been redeemed by the blood of the Cross. As a result healing, deliverance, salvation, and righteousness, have been transferred to all who will receive the work of Jesus, through identification with Him—by receiving Him as Lord and Savior.

Look at Isaiah 53:4-5 which explains what Jesus has done for us through the Cross, "⁴Surely He has borne our griefs and carried our sorrows; yet we esteemed Him stricken, smitten by God, and afflicted. ⁵But He was wounded for our transgressions, He was bruised for our iniquities; the chastisement for our peace was upon Him, and by His stripes we are healed."

The Easy to Read Version says, "⁴The fact is, it was our suffering He took on himself; He bore our pain. But we thought that God was punishing Him, that God was beating Him for something He did. ⁵But He was being punished for what we did. He was crushed because of our guilt. He took the punishment we deserved, and this brought us peace. We were healed because of His pain."

The (God's Word Translation) declares, "⁴He certainly has taken upon himself our suffering and carried our sorrows, but we thought that God had wounded Him, beat Him, and punished Him. ⁵He was wounded for our rebellious acts. He was crushed for our sins. He was punished so that we could have peace, and we received healing from his wounds."

MICHAEL VIDAURRI, D. MIN.

Everything you and I could ever want has been made available to us through Jesus death on the Cross. We have been given back the authority which was originally intended for man. We have been made the Righteousness of God in Christ (See 2 Corinthians 5:21).

We have been freed from the bondage of fear (See Romans 8:15). And we have also been given the gift of healing through the stripes, bruises, and beatings which Jesus took on His back before He died on the Cross. If you need healing, if you need deliverance from anything that the devil is using to keep you in bondage, don't allow it to remain in your life anymore.

Break the devils stronghold through the use of Jesus' name, by applying the blood of the Cross to your situation, as the anointing which removes every burden and destroys every yoke. Recognize and receive the SON OF RIGHTEOUSNESS WHO HAS COME WITH HEALING IN HIS WINGS — AND BE MADE WHOLE — TODAY !

Daily Declaration

Father, I thank You for Jesus — the Sun of Righteousness who has come with healing in His wings. He has come as the Light of this world to remove and deliver me from the bondage of Sin. I gladly receive all that You came to do for me Jesus! I receive You Jesus, as my Lord and Savior. I believe that You died for me and paid the complete price for every one of my sins — past — present — and future. Please forgive me Jesus. Teach me to live like You, to love like You, to forgive like You, and to draw others to You so that they can receive this same FREEDOM!

I bless You Lord, and pray these things in Jesus' name, Amen.

Day 28
What's Your Life's Composition: Drama, Horror, Mystery, Or Adventure?

"My heart is overflowing with a good theme; I recite my composition concerning the King; my tongue is the pen of a ready writer."

Psalm 45:1

Have you ever been around a person who was continually depressed or negative? If so, what was the first thing you wanted to do? Every time I'm around someone like that, my first response is to try to change the atmosphere by finding something positive to focus on, by reminding that person what the Word of God has to say concerning who they are in Jesus and what they have access to in Him. But if that doesn't work, my next response is to pray with them and then leave.

Life is too short to stay negative. And for me, hanging around negative people is like being infected by poison oak or poison ivy: it is quick to spread and leaves an annoying irritation in its wake.

Have you ever thought of your life as a song, a play, or maybe even a novel? I love how the psalmist refers to his life in Psalm 45:1. He says that his life is overflowing with a good theme...I like that. It's positive and He can focus on the good things that are happening to him even in the midst of the bad.

The Hebrew word translated as overflowing in the English, is the word: *rachash*, which means to be stirred up, to flow over the brim, to be very full of something.

The Hebrew word translated as theme, is the word *davar* which translated as speech, words, acts, or agreement.

Those are two very important words that we must pay close attention to in order to understand what the psalmist is trying to convey to us here. If we were to rewrite that verse we might say, "My inner man is stirred up and running over with joyful and agreeable speech and actions."

The Psalmist then goes on to say, "I recite my composition concerning the King." In other words, He is saying that he is testifying or decreeing what God has already declared about his life. He is building himself up in faith. He is stirring up the gift inside of him — releasing God's promises over himself and changing the course of his life.

This is crucial! You and I may be surrounded by negative circumstances all around us, demanding our attention, but the important truth is that we are going through them! We are not wallowing in the mud, camping out, or staying there forever — it is a temporary situation!

In order to get out of those negative circumstances we must turn our focus from the problem that we face to the solution that we have in Jesus.

We must begin to SPEAK — to DECLARE — and to RECITE the will and Word of the King — thereby ACTING upon His promises. By doing so, we can't help but begin to run over with a good theme — joy, peace, hope, and ultimately agreement with God and the precious promises found in the Bible.

Just like Isaiah 43:25-26 suggests, we are to put God in remembrance of His promises. We are to agree with what He has already spoken and declared for our lives. We are to state our case and be acquitted. This is for our benefit. To stir ourselves up in the Word, remembering what God has promised to us, and then acting on what we confidently know is His will for our lives!

When we know the promises of God we can build our case against the devil. We put him on notification that he is in direct violation of the Law and that he is trespassing onto holy ground.

W immediately serve him notice declaring that he has no legal grounds to steal, kill, and destroy anything that belongs to us. Then God, who is our just judge, reads the verdict for our case: "I find the plaintiff (YOU and Me), free from every effect of the Curse. And I find the defendants (Satan and his demonic goons), guilty and in contempt of court! And as the Supreme Judge of Heaven and Earth, I order Satan to pay restitution to the plaintiff — 7 times what he has stolen and the substance of his house."

Proverbs 6:31 (KJV) declares, "But if he [a thief] be found, he shall restore sevenfold; he shall give all the substance of his house."

Satan not only has to return what he has stolen from you, but he must also add to it. That is what recompense is all about — it is payment with interest.

The final portion of this verse says, "My tongue is the pen of a ready writer." The word translated tongue is the Hebrew word *lashon* which means tongue or language. The words ready writer are translated from the Hebrew words, *mahir saphar*, which mean a quick and expert scribe or declarer.

In other words, his tongue is the stylus or the instrument of a quick and expert speaker of the promises of God. He knows precisely what God has promised to him, and he will not settle for anything less. He quickly and accurately notifies Satan when he has overstepped his boundaries and commands him to retreat or face the consequences of God's wrath.

The Old Testament prophet Ezra was such a man. Ezra 7:6 says, "This Ezra came up from Babylon; and he was a skilled scribe in the Law of Moses, which the LORD God of Israel had given. The king granted him all his requests, according to the hand of the LORD his God upon him."

When you know the Word because you know your God, then you have no choice but to succeed. The hand of God is for you and opens doors that no man can shut and shuts doors that no man can open (See Revelation 3:7-8).

Just as the psalmist instructed us in Psalm 45:1, we are to be stirred up and running over in the inner man (in our spirit), with joyful and agreeable speech and actions. You may be asking yourself the question: *Agreeable with what?* Agreeable with the Bible – the Bible must become the final authority for our lives! We must learn to mold our lives to fit the truth of the Bible not the Bible to fit the actions of our lives. We must begin speaking and reciting the will of God (which is the Word of God), in its totality, putting the devil on notice when he is trying to mess with any of our affairs.

Just because you may have received a bad report from your doctor, your accountant, your spouse, etc., that doesn't mean you have to accept it and lie down and die. No! That's when you STAND FIRM and begin declaring the truth of the Word even more boldly than ever before. The Word of God has the power to transform the reality you are facing into the Blessing of God.

2 Corinthians 4:18 is our example of this truth, "While we do not look at the things which are seen, but at the things which are not seen [God's Promises]. For the things which are seen are temporary, but the things which are not seen are eternal."

Quit focusing on the negative! Quit commenting on the temporary! Instead, become a quick and expert declarer of the Word of Truth.

The only way you can do that is by knowing your Bible and the promises within. When you learn who you are in Christ and what belongs to you by covenant right, you become marked for success. You are set-up to write YOUR masterpiece. You become the next one in line for a number one best seller which everyone will want to read and hear.

You don't have time to be putting up with drama, tragedy, horror, or blues. And you were never designed to do so. You only have the time to focus on the Great Adventure that God has designed and created for you to experience. Don't allow the enemy to put you on the sidelines or to delay the great plans God has designed for your life. It's time to begin writing your story, singing your song, acting out your play, and doing it to the GLORY and WILL of Almighty God!

Daily Declaration

Father I declare that my life will be a Blessing to all who come in contact with me. I refuse to be sidelined by the devil. I refuse to allow fear, grief, drama, blues, tragedy, or any other aspect of the Curse keep me from enjoying Your best—in Jesus' name. Today, I start fresh. Today, I begin a new chapter—the beginning of the best days I've ever lived up until this point. I fully expect each new day to be better than the day before. When trouble comes my way, I will briefly stop, serve the devil notice, and then continue right along as I had before in Your perfect Peace and Favor.

Thank You Jesus for giving me Your overcoming peace, authority, and life. I am truly more than a conqueror in You. Because of You, I am free to live and enjoy life to its fullest potential. You promised, "I came that they may have and enjoy life, and have it in abundance (to the full, till it overflows)." (John 10:10, AMP). I believe and I receive that abundant life today—In Jesus' mighty name, Amen!

Day 29
God's Got A Hold Of You

"...He [God] Himself has said, I will not in any way fail you nor give you up nor leave you without support. [I will] not, [I will] not, [I will] not in any degree leave you helpless nor forsake nor let [you] down (relax My hold on you)! [Assuredly not!]"

Hebrews 13:5 (AMP)

I know that it's sometimes hard for new believers and even those who have been Christians for decades to truly cast their cares upon God. It can be difficult to hand our cares and concerns over to a person we have never seen with our natural eyes.

In fact, sometimes we may mistakenly view God in the same way we do our friends and family members. Because of our ignorance, we may think that He will let us down like they have. But I can promise you from the Word of God and from personal experience that He will never let you down. He will always come through for you if you do what He has commanded you to do and if you will step out in faith trusting that He will do what He's promised to do.

The Bible talks about two types of friends one who will leave you, lie to you, and hurt you, and another who will stand by you, through thick and thin, and remain forever loyal.

Proverbs 18:24 (AMP) says, "The man of many friends [a friend of all the world] will prove himself a bad friend, but there is a friend who sticks closer than a brother."

In John 15:13 (AMP) We are shown what a great friend we have in Jesus, "No one has greater love [no one has shown stronger affection] than to lay down (give up) his own life for his friends." Jesus gave it all for us—Now that's not only friendship—That's LOVE!

You see, God's love for us is so much stronger than that of our earthly friends; He receives glory in bringing us through our battles victoriously. He takes joy in going before us and behind us and defeating our enemies. He isn't afraid of a little scuffle with the devil—he takes pride in being our God who is mighty to save!

Let's look at a few Scriptures that prove this truth:

Isaiah 41:13 tells us, "For I, the LORD your God, will hold your right hand, saying to you, 'Fear not, I will help you."

Isaiah 45:1-2 (NLT) says, "2 This is what the LORD says: 'I will go before you (insert your name), and level the mountains. I will smash down gates of bronze and cut through bars of iron. 3 And I will give you treasures hidden in the darkness— secret riches. I will do this so you may know that I am the LORD, the God of Israel, the one who calls you by name.'"

Psalm 5:11-12 declares, "11 But let all those rejoice who put their trust in You; Let them ever shout for joy, because You defend them; let those also who love Your name be joyful in You. 12 For You, O LORD, will bless the righteous; with favor You will surround him as with a shield."

In Deuteronomy 31:6, 8 God told Moses, "⁶ Be strong and of good courage, do not fear nor be afraid of them; for the LORD your God, He is the One who goes with you. He will not leave you nor forsake you… ⁸ And the LORD, He is the One who goes before you. He will be with you, He will not leave you nor forsake you; do not fear nor be dismayed."

Just like He said this to Moses, He is saying the same thing to you as you go into your battle—He won't leave you or forsake you. He's sticking with you closer than a brother. And He's got a tight hold on you, so fear not!

I absolutely love the way the Amplified Bible explains God's commitment to us in Hebrews 13:5, "[God] Himself has said, I will not in any way fail you nor give you up nor leave you without support. [I will] not, [I will] not, [I will] not in any degree leave you helpless nor forsake nor let [you] down (relax My hold on you)! [Assuredly not!]"

Do you see that? It's just like Jesus telling His disciples, "Verily, Verily," or "Assuredly, Assuredly I tell you." This is the most solemn vow that God can make and He wants us to know how serious He is about it.

But He doesn't stop there! He continues by saying: I will not, I will not, I will not leave you helpless, forsake you, or relax my hold on you!

I love that! That is the love of our Heavenly Father, to comfort us and to chase away every ounce of fear and doubt that would try to creep in to convince us otherwise.

If you have made God your Lord, your Source, and your Protector—YOU have absolutely nothing to fear! He has got a tight hold on you and all that concerns you. He's never letting go. He's not like any other person you have ever known before. His promises are eternal and He'll never break them for any reason.

God is honored to be the God of your life and He takes His job seriously. In fact, look at what He said about you in Psalm 91:14-16, "14 Because he has set his love upon Me, therefore I will deliver him; I will set him on high, because he has known My name. 15 He shall call upon Me, and I will answer him; I will be with him in trouble; I will deliver him and honor him. 16 With long life I will satisfy him, and show him My salvation."

Now that's Good News! Praise God!

Daily Declaration

Thank You Lord for being someone I can always trust and rely upon. I know that everything You have promised to me You will surely do. Your Word will never return void, but it will accomplish what You sent it to perform. I rest peacefully in the understanding of who I am in Jesus. I am the redeemed, the Blessed, the Prosperous, the Healed, the Strong, the Wise, the Good-looking, and the one who always Overcomes in You! You are my God in whom I trust.

Thank You Father, for always taking hold of me and protecting me from harms grasp. Thank You for hiding me in the Secret Place of the Most High God. I am so thankful that You stick closer to me than a brother—You are my wonderful and loving Daddy. I praise You Lord for Your unfailing love and pray these things in Jesus' name, Amen.

Day 30
From Everlasting To Everlasting

"[17] But the mercy of the LORD is from everlasting to everlasting on those who fear Him, and His righteousness to children's children, [18] to such as keep His covenant, and to those who remember His commandments to do them."

Psalm 103:17-18

D o you understand the difference between the mercy and the grace of God? It may sound like a simple question; however, many people confuse the two or use them interchangeably without really comprehending the difference. You could make a similar case for the words omnipotence and sovereignty—but there is a distinct difference between the two.

The word mercy comes from the Hebrew word *chesed*, which focuses on God's: goodness, His kindness, His deeds of devotion and loyalty, His loving-kindness, covenant love, and steadfast faithfulness. This word is also often used to describe covenant characteristics of a marriage (See Hosea 2:19), and dealings of faithfulness based on oaths which are made between two people (See Genesis 47:29 and 2 Samuel 10:2).

The word grace is translated from the Hebrew word *chen*, which refers to special favor, adornment, charm, acceptance, and it deals with receiving both approval and provision due to requests which are made of someone.

Grace is literally an act that is performed for another regardless of how the grantor of that grace feels towards the recipient of that grace. The giver of grace may not have pleasant feelings towards the one he showers with grace, but it is again based on his/her covenant relationship with the one receiving that grace.

The main distinction between these mercy and grace, is that Mercy is God responding in covenant faithfulness without having been asked for special treatment or favor. Whereas, Grace has to do with God's covenant approval and provision for those who request help from Him.

Both of these responses from God are based on His character and His covenant relationship to man. It is easy to see why these words are so often confused and used interchangeably.

One of the greatest illustrations of Mercy has to do with faithfulness to an oath which was made between two people.

In Genesis 47:27-31 we find Jacob [Israel], receiving mercy from his son Joseph who has become second in command throughout all Egypt. "[27] So Israel dwelt in the land of Egypt, in the country of Goshen; and they had possessions there and grew and multiplied exceedingly. [28] And Jacob lived in the land of Egypt seventeen years. So the length of Jacob's life was one hundred and forty-seven years. [29] When the time drew near that Israel [Jacob] must die, he called his son Joseph and said to him, "Now if I have found favor [Mercy] in your sight, please put your hand under my thigh, and deal kindly and truly with me. Please do not bury me in Egypt, [30] but let me lie with my fathers; you shall carry me out of Egypt and bury me in their burial place." And he said, "I will do as you have said." [31] Then he said, "Swear to me." And he swore to him. So Israel [Jacob] bowed himself on the head of the bed."

Out of mercy to his father's request, because of the covenant made to his father, Joseph's descendants moved Jacob's bones out of Egypt and buried them back in the Promised Land. Covenant promises are unbreakable in the sight of God and those who follow Him.

In 2 Samuel Chapter 9, we witness another illustration of mercy being demonstrated by David towards Jonathan's son Mephibosheth, who had nothing after his father and grandfather King Saul were dead.

Mephibosheth was a cripple and His grandfather Saul had just been defeated by David and his armies. He would have been destined to live as a peasant or die a cruel and painful death from starvation because he couldn't provide for himself.

In 2 Samuel 9:1-7 (NKJV) we read, "Now David said, "Is there still anyone who is left of the house of Saul, that I may show him kindness [Mercy] for Jonathan's sake?" [2] And there was a servant of the house of Saul whose name was Ziba. So when they had called him to David, the king said to him, "Are you Ziba?" He said, "At your service!" [3] Then the king said, "Is there not still someone of the house of Saul, to whom I may show the kindness of God?" And Ziba said to the king, "There is still a son of Jonathan who is lame in his feet." [4] So the king said to him, "Where is he?" And Ziba said to the king, "Indeed he is in the house of Machir the son of Ammiel, in Lo Debar." [5] Then King David sent and brought him out of the house of Machir the son of Ammiel, from Lo Debar. [6] Now when Mephibosheth the son of Jonathan, the son of Saul, had come to David, he fell on his face and prostrated himself. Then David said, "Mephibosheth?" And he answered, "Here is your servant!" ⁷ So David said to him, "Do not fear, for I will surely show you kindness [Mercy] for Jonathan your father's sake, and will restore to you all the land of Saul your grandfather; and you shall eat bread at my table continually."

It is interesting that in verse 5, we read that David had Mephibosheth brought to him from a place called *Lo Debar*. The words *Lo Debar*, translated from the Hebrew, literally mean: from no thing or no word.

In other words, this man had nothing, he had no reason to live, but because of David's mercy, he had a continual seat at the king's table.

Psalm 25:4-7 declares, "Show me Your ways, O LORD; teach me Your paths. ⁵ Lead me in Your truth and teach me, for You are the God of my salvation; on You I wait all the day. ⁶ Remember, O LORD, Your tender mercies and Your loving-kindnesses, for they are from of old. ⁷ Do not remember the sins of my youth, nor my transgressions; according to Your mercy remember me, for Your goodness' sake, O LORD."

In this passage it is evident that God is acting out of covenant mercy to forgive and to forget the psalmist's sins and to deliver him from his troubles.

Luke 6:35-36 is another illustration of mercy, which always responds in kindness even when it is not deserved. "³⁵ But love your enemies, do good, and lend, hoping for nothing in return; and your reward will be great, and you will be sons of the Most High. For He is kind to the unthankful and evil. ³⁶ Therefore be merciful, just as your Father also is merciful."

Mercy is an act of love which is performed for another's benefit, despite how they have acted towards you. God loves us and was merciful towards us even when we didn't have a relationship with Him.

Romans 5:7-8 declares, "⁷ Very rarely will anyone die for a righteous person, though for a good person someone might possibly dare to die. ⁸ But God demonstrates his own love for us in this: While we were still sinners, Christ died for us."

We didn't deserve anything! We didn't earn anything! And we never will! Yet in His great mercy, God sent Jesus to die for us and to restore the relationship between us and Himself. NOW THAT IS AMAZING LOVE!

It is important for us to always remember that God is for us even when we act like fools. He loves us and responds to us in kindness and covenant faithfulness because that is simply who He is and what He has promised to do.

God is continually loyal to us demonstrating the fruit of His promises to us, because everything He does is **_ALWAYS_** in line with the covenant He has made to us in the Bible.

When the enemy tries to convince us that we have blown it beyond God's grace and forgiveness — When he lies saying that our sins because of the sins are unforgiveable — we must always remember that God's mercy is from everlasting to everlasting.

We must remember that He is always looking to move us out of *Lo Debar* [our place of nothing and no word, into a place of BLESSING]. Into a place where we can sit at the KING'S TABLE!

It's high time for us to believe and act on Psalm 23:6 which says, "Surely goodness and mercy shall follow me all the days of my life; and I will dwell in the house of the LORD forever." Agree with that promise and receive it for your life today. HIS MERCY ENDURES FOREVER! PRAISE GOD!

Daily Declaration

I declare that I walk in the grace (the unmerited favor) and the mercy of Almighty God. Lord You promised in Psalm 23:6 (AMP), "Surely or only goodness, mercy, and unfailing love shall follow me all the days of my life, and through the length of my days the house of the Lord [and His presence] shall be my dwelling place." This is Your will and Your plan for my life, and I receive it by faith.

I am grateful that just like Mephibosheth You have taken me out of *Lo Debar* (a place of nothing), and seated me with Jesus in Heavenly places. (See Ephesians 2:6). You have seated me at the King of kings table and offered me everything You have to offer. Moreover, You have delivered me from the bondage and slavery of sin—HALLELUJAH!

Thank You Father for loving me in spite of my shortcomings, I could never earn Your love or my salvation, but it is through Your mercy (through Jesus), that I inherit Your promises. I am in awe of Your covenant love towards me. I bless You, praise Your name, and receive the gift of love and salvation (Complete wholeness that You've given me in Jesus. I pray these things in Jesus' name, Amen!

Day 31
Building Yourself Up On Your Most Holy Faith

"¹⁷ But you, beloved, remember the words which were spoken before by the apostles of our Lord Jesus Christ: ¹⁸ how they told you that there would be mockers in the last time who would walk according to their own ungodly lusts. ¹⁹ These are sensual persons, who cause divisions, not having the Spirit. ²⁰ But you, beloved, building yourselves up on your most holy faith, praying in the Holy Spirit, ²¹ keep yourselves in the love of God, looking for the mercy of our Lord Jesus Christ unto eternal life."

Jude 1:17-21

Over the years there has been a lot of confusion about speaking in tongues or praying in the Holy Ghost. The devil has used confusion regarding spiritual gifts to cause division and strife within the Church and to destroy relationships through ignorance and bullheadedness.

Strife is a cancer, in fact, Satan uses strife regularly because he knows just how powerful of a force it can be. In Matthew 12:25 Jesus said, "Every kingdom divided against itself is brought to desolation, and every city or house divided against itself will not stand."

Satan knows that if he can get Christians fighting over frivolous things, there will be no unity, there will be no real power, and there will be no threat to his kingdom. As a result of giving him a foothold in our lives, he can then sneak in and steal, kill, and destroy those things most precious to us while we argue over nonsensical things like whether speaking in tongues is really a spiritual gift from God or if it's from the devil.

I remember as a kid in the Baptist church, I heard things like, "Tongues are from the devil," or "Speaking in tongue is the devil's language."

I was terrified by the thought that I might speak in tongues and say something that would damn me to hell. But that fear was unjustified because the Holy Spirit doesn't possess people like demons. But I was ignorant about the Holy Spirit because we didn't talk about Him in my church except for referring to Him as "it."

And the pastors NEVER spoke about tongues other than to say negative things about those who operated in these gifts. The first time I visited a church where people spoke in tongues, I thought everyone was possessed by the devil. That was what I had been taught in my denomination.

But the truth was the people who said these things, were just as ignorant about the Bible as I was. They were judging entire denominations/groups solely on the basis of Man's traditions instead of what the Bible had to say about this spiritual gift.

In 1 Corinthians 12:1-3 Paul writes, "Now concerning spiritual gifts, brethren, I do not want you to be ignorant: [2] You know that you were Gentiles, carried away to these dumb idols, however you were led. [3] ***Therefore I make known to you that no one speaking by the Spirit of God calls Jesus accursed, and no one can say that Jesus is Lord except by the Holy Spirit.***" (Emphasis Added).

Do you see that? If I had known what the Bible had to say about tongues, it would have relieved all of my fears.

The Holy Spirit never comes in as an unwelcomed guest and He never makes you say anything that is unscriptural or of the devil. The Holy Spirit, just like Jesus, only says and does what He hears the Father say and do. (See John 5:19 and John 12:49).

The Apostle Paul explains the gift of tongues in greater detail. In 1 Corinthians 14:2-5 we read, "[2] For he who speaks in a tongue does not speak to men but to God, for no one understands him; however, in the spirit he speaks mysteries. [3] But he who prophesies speaks edification and exhortation and comfort to men. [4] He who speaks in a tongue edifies himself, but he who prophesies edifies the church. [5] I wish you all spoke with tongues, but even more that you prophesied; for he who prophesies is greater than he who speaks with tongues, unless indeed he interprets, that the church may receive edification."

Paul tells us exactly what the gift of tongues is for in this passage. In fact, he says that he wished that all believers spoke in tongues for one reason — to build themselves up. What does it mean to build yourself up?

Notice what Paul instructed Timothy to do in 2 Timothy 1:6-7, "[6] Therefore I remind you to stir up the gift of God which is in you through the laying on of my hands. [7] For God has not given us a spirit of fear, but of power and of love and of a sound mind."

The Spirit of God lives inside each of us and Romans 10:17 explains that faith comes by hearing the Word. When we get into our prayer closets and pray in other tongues, it builds faith within us. The Holy Spirit begins operating in unison with our spirit man and helps us to pray for the things we don't know how to pray for.

He encourages our spirit man to move forward into faith and to overcome the obstacles that are trying to stand between us and our victory.

The gift of tongues is a power gift. It clears our spirit from the clutter of the world and builds us up in faith to move into greater victories.

I Corinthians 14:2 says, "For he who speaks in a tongue does not speak to men but to God, for no one understands him; however, in the spirit he speaks mysteries."

When people are praying in tongues they are speaking directly to God and God is revealing mysteries or secrets to them through His Holy Spirit. The person speaking may not even understand what he is praying—from a cognitive perspective—but his spirit man understands and receives direction and encouragement from the throne of heaven.

Paul explains to us in 1 Corinthians 14:6, that in corporate worship he would rather that the Church prophesy instead of pray in tongues. He says this because prophesy is given by God as a tool to build up the entire church—through common language which everyone can understand.

Even though Paul encourages us to prophesy, He doesn't say to throw the gift of tongues away—it has great value. Tongues builds up the individual whereas prophesy builds up the corporate body. Therefore, he suggests that when we get together to worship as the Church, the gift of prophesy is used so that everyone present can benefit.

In 1 Corinthians 2:12-15 Paul says, "[12] Now we have received, not the spirit of the world, but the Spirit who is from God, that we might know the things that have been freely given to us by God. [13] These things we also speak, not in words which man's wisdom teaches but which the Holy Spirit teaches, comparing spiritual things with spiritual. [14] But the natural man does not receive the things of the Spirit of God, for they are foolishness to him; nor can he know them, because they are spiritually discerned. [15] But he who is spiritual judges all things, yet he himself is rightly judged by no one."

This is another reason why Paul instruct the church to use prophesy in corporate worship over tongues. Just like I was freaked out as a kid when others were speaking in tongues around me and I didn't understand what was happening, those people who visit our churches for the first time and are not familiar with this ministry gift may become scared or even turned off too.

They may interpret it from a carnal perspective and see it as foolishness. As unbelievers or even as Christians who have not matured in the things of the Bible, they may not have learned to interpret spiritual things by the Spirit of God as 1 Corinthians 2:13 describes.

In the book of Jude we read, "[18] how they told you that there would be mockers in the last time who would walk according to their own ungodly lusts. [19] These are sensual persons, who cause divisions, not having the Spirit. [20] But you, beloved, building yourselves up on your most holy faith, praying in the Holy Spirit, [21] keep yourselves in the love of God, looking for the mercy of our Lord Jesus Christ unto eternal life." (Jude 1:18-21).

Jude tells us that in the last days there will be mockers of God, mockers of the Bible, mockers of everything that has to do with Jesus and real Bible faith. The devil is always looking to cause division and strife within the Body of Christ, because he wants us to be powerless against him.

In Jude 1:20-21 we read, "[20] But you, beloved, ***BUILDING YOURSELVES UP ON YOUR MOST HOLY FAITH, PRAYING IN THE HOLY SPIRIT,*** [21] keep yourselves in the love of God, looking for the mercy of our Lord Jesus Christ unto eternal life." (Emphasis Added).

There will always be those who don't believe certain parts of the Bible. There will also be those who believe, but choose not to operate in all that is available to them. That's their right, because they have a free will.

The important thing to understand however, is that Jude tells us that we are to BUILD OURSELVES UP IN OUR MOST HOLY FAITH—PRAYING IN THE SPIRIT. It's not a suggestion—it's an order.

Why does Jude call praying in the Spirit, "Praying in our "most holy faith?" I like to think about it like this: God has great plans for each of us. Plans to BLESS us, plans to help us succeed, plans to prosper us and to move us from faith to faith and glory to glory (See 2 Corinthians 3:17-17 and Romans 1:17).

But in order for Him to do this, He sometimes needs to change our thinking. He may ask us to believe Him for things which seem impossible to our rational mind. Things that are TOO BIG to wrap our minds and our faith around and believe. But the good news is He has given us the mind of Christ (See 1 Corinthians 2:16 and Philippians 2:5-6).

So, in order to accomplish His goals through us, God sometimes needs to pray through us without our rational mind interfering. In these circumstances He uses the Holy Spirit to encourage us to speak things out of our mouths, which we don't understand with our rational mind.

Romans 8:26-27 says it this way, "[26] Likewise the Spirit also helps in our weaknesses. For we do not know what we should pray for as we ought, but the Spirit Himself makes intercession for us with groanings [sounds or speaking], which cannot be uttered [understood in a natural language]. [27] Now He who searches the hearts knows what the mind of the Spirit is, because He makes intercession for the saints according to the will of God."

The Holy Spirit helps us by encouraging us to pray in our Holy language. He encourages us to agree with God's will through speaking in tongues. Yet at the same time, even though our natural minds may not understand what we are speaking, our spirit understands and agrees with Him by faith and together we agree with the will of God for our lives.

This agreement is the same agreement which we see illustrated in Matthew 18:19-20, which states, "[19] Again I say to you that if two of you agree on earth concerning anything that they ask, it will be done for them by My Father in heaven. [20] For where two or three are gathered together in My name, I am there in the midst of them."

This agreement causes the thing we have just prayed to begin the process of manifestation. Our natural reasoning, because it is not involved in this spiritual process, cannot then get in the way to block this plan of God from coming to pass.

That's because we're not being double minded or speaking faith but operating in doubt.

James speaks of this James 1:5-8. There is no wishy-washy, back and forth between faith and unbelief, and as Mark 9:23 clearly illustrates, "If you can believe, all things are possible to him who believes."

This is the reason that I believe Paul, Jude, Peter, John, and the entire church that was born in Acts Chapter 2, believed and operated in the gift of tongues. God uses this gift to help us achieve great things in the Kingdom.

God won't make you do anything that you don't want to do—because He has given you a free will. God is a gentleman. He's not like the devil—He doesn't come in uninvited and possess men like Satan tries to do. He only comes when He is invited by us.

You don't ever have to speak in tongues if you don't want to! You don't have to experience things beyond your wildest imagination if you don't want to. That doesn't make you any less of a Christian or any less important to the Body of Christ. But if you are anything like me, you want all that God has for you. You want to be used to do great exploits for God and His Kingdom. You want to operate in your MOST HOLY FAITH—and to begin seeing the mountains that are trying to stand in your way being removed and cast into the sea.

Mark 11:22-24 declares, "22 So Jesus answered and said to them, "Have faith in God.23 For assuredly, I say to you, whoever says to this mountain, 'Be removed and be cast into the sea,' and does not doubt in his heart, but believes that those things he says will be done, he will have whatever he says.24 Therefore I say to you, whatever things you ask when you pray, believe that you receive them, and you will have them."

If you're anything like me, anything like the Apostle Paul and the multitudes of believers who have accomplished great things by allowing God to operate through them.

Don't allow fear of the unknown or your ignorance of the Word stop you from reaching your greatest potential. Learn the Word of God and then BUILD YOURSELF UP IN YOUR MOST HOLY FAITH!

Daily Declaration

Father, I thank You for the Holy Spirit and I receive by faith everything that You have for me. Lord, teach me Your Word. Lead me by Your Spirit. And teach me Your truth. I refuse to operate in ignorance or to do things just for the sake of doing them. I want to know why I am doing what I do. There has to be a rhyme and reason to it or it's only vain tradition.

Father, give me the gift of tongues. I pray for Your Spirit to come upon me and to speak through me in Jesus' name. I open my mouth willingly and begin to speak the words that You put into my spirit. I bind fear, intimidation, and doubt now in Jesus' name. I receive all that You have for me in Jesus' mighty name.

A NOTE:

Now spend time speaking those words that are coming into your spirit right now. There is NOTHING to fear. If it sounds foreign to you — that's alright — everything takes practice. Just allow the Holy Spirit to speak through you. Go back over and study the Scripture in today's devotion and meditate on those things they say. Then ask God to reveal to you what you are saying and He will. I pray God's Blessing and His supernatural favour over you in Jesus' mighty name, Amen!

FOLLOW US AS WE FOLLOW JESUS

On the web at:
www.michaelvidaurri.com

On Facebook at:
https://www.facebook.com/pages/Michael-Vidaurri-Ministries/361809073932887

On Twitter at:
https://twitter.com/mike_vidaurri

On LinkedIn at:
http://www.linkedin.com/pub/michael-vidaurri-d-min/66/36a/b6

24401509R00124

Made in the USA
Columbia, SC
23 August 2018